SHOT BY SHOT

A Practical Guide to Filmmaking

FOURTH EDITION

Shot 1: 10s
shot 2: 25s
shark: 15s
shft: 45s
end: 20s

by

John Cantine ~ Susan Howard ~ Brady Lewis

PITTSBURGH FILMMAKERS
THE MEDIA ARTS CENTER

Illustrations: Jennifer E. Merriman, Andrew Sproule and Adam Sultanov

Photographs: Richard Kelly

Design/Layout: Gern Roberts

Cover image: *A Trip to the Moon* (1902) by Georges Melies

A Trip to the Moon (cover) and Muybridge motion study (pg. 7):
The Museum of Modern Art/Film Stills Archive

ISBN 978-0-9637433-8-1

Published by:
Pittsburgh Filmmakers
477 Melwood Ave.
Pittsburgh, PA 15213
pghfilmmakers.org

Table of Contents

Preface

Motion picture production has changed dramatically since the third edition of *Shot by Shot: A Practical Guide to Filmmaking* was published. Most student projects shot on film are now transferred immediately to digital files, edited on a computer and released on video. Professional film productions, too, are almost entirely edited digitally, regardless of whether they are released on film, in digital form or both. Solid-state technology allows video cameras to act more like film cameras. If you have a film background, swapping out P2 cards can't help but remind you of changing film magazines.

This new edition of *Shot by Shot* has been extensively revised to reflect these changes. We have added a new chapter on video cameras and the process of recording video. The editing chapter has been expanded to include digital and hybrid workflows. We have added a chapter that attempts to sum up the current opportunities for exhibition and distribution. We have included new examples from recent feature films that reflect changing styles and aesthetics. Every chapter has been extensively revised to bring the book up to date with current technology and techniques.

At the same time, we have retained much of the original information for those who have fallen in love with the analog processes of flatbed editors and magnetic fullcoat or those teachers who believe that the traditional methods of film production instill a discipline that serves young filmmakers well, whatever technology they have at their disposal. We have also retained the easy readability and straightforward explanations that many readers found useful in the earlier editions and that we feel are even more valuable amid the acronym-filled technical jargon of 21st century motion picture production.

We have tried to be thorough in introducing and discussing important basic concepts of filmmaking, but it was never our intention to go into great technical detail in any specific area. There are other good books available that go into much greater detail, and we use some of them in our advanced classes. We have tried to introduce filmmaking concepts and language in a practical, understandable way. Each new film term is set in boldface and is defined within the body of the text the first time it appears. A concise definition of each boldfaced term can be found in the glossary. "Pre-Production" is the ninth chapter in the book, and while an argument could be made for discussing it before anything else, it is impossible to outline the concepts of good pre-production without first having an understanding of the terms, details and potential pitfalls involved in shooting and editing.

We would like to thank our friends and colleagues who have helped us in this effort. Richard Kelly shot all the photographs, as he has done for each edition of this book. Gern Roberts did the layout for the fourth edition. Adam Sultanov created new illustrations for this edition. Jessica Futrell created the Index. Others who have helped us and deserve thanks include Dean Mougianis, Kathleen Rebel, Catherine Gimbrone, Kate Knorr, Gary Kaboly, Gus Samios, Merging Media and Charlie Humphrey. We thank all of them plus the entire staff of Pittsburgh Filmmakers for indulging us in this on-going project.

Brady Lewis ~ Susan Howard ~ John Cantine
July 2011

Chapter 1

The Moving Image

At about the time inventors began to perfect the photographic process in the late nineteenth century, they also began to consider techniques by which they could photographically reproduce motion. Late eighteenth and nineteenth-century parlor toys, such as flip books and the zoetrope, demonstrated that the human eye seemed to retain the impression of an image slightly longer than it was actually exposed to that image. In the 1820's this phenomenon was dubbed **persistence of vision**. Its basic principles theorized that when a series of images are presented in rapid succession, the eye "blurs" them into one image; if there are very small differences in position from one image to the next, the brain will perceive movement; the images have to be presented quickly in order to be perceived as movement rather than as a series of still images. This explanation for the illusion of motion was accepted for many years. We now explain this phenomenon in slightly different terms.

If a series of fixed images are projected onto a screen in succession, with slight differences between them, the illusion of movement can be created on the screen. If an image is presented to the human eye, removed, and then returned quickly enough, the human eye and brain see the image as being constant. This phenomenon is known as **flicker fusion**. If, for instance, images are flashed on a screen at a rate of twenty or more per second, the eye sees one constant image.

In addition, if one image is slightly different from the previous image, a person viewing the sequence will see the illusion of smooth, continuous motion. Imagine a series of images beginning with a circle at the left edge of the screen, a second image that shows the circle slightly to the right of that position and so on until the circle is at the right edge of the screen. If these images are shown in succession, and the increments of change are small enough, a viewer watching them will perceive not different images of circles, but a single circle moving from the left edge of the screen to the right edge. This is referred to as the **short-range motion phenomenon**.

Flicker fusion, along with the short-range motion phenomenon, makes film and video presentation possible. During a film screening many thousands of photographic images run through a movie projector, which shines light through them. These images are focused onto a white or silver screen, creating the moving images the audience sees. Video uses different technology to turn light into an electrical signal. Video monitors then turn this signal into a series of images that create the illusion of movement on a screen.

The Film Image

A motion sequence photographed by Eadweard Muybridge.

In the 1870's Eadweard Muybridge successfully demonstrated the photographic reproduction of motion when he set up a row of still cameras and photographed a racehorse running past them. When viewed in rapid succession these images provided a graphic example of photographed motion. However, setting up a series of still cameras to capture a second or two of action was not a practical method of photographing motion, and inventors worked to develop a camera that would rapidly expose a series of sequential images onto a single strip of film.

A breakthrough in the development of the movie camera occurred with the invention of flexible celluloid film stock, which replaced the cumbersome glass plates previously used to capture light and create the photographic image. In 1888 George Eastman marketed the first celluloid film. The flexible strip of film had **sprocket holes**, or **perforations**, along its edges. Inside the camera the teeth of **sprocket wheels** engaged these perforations, moving the film through the camera. In 1890 William Dickson and Thomas Edison successfully tested a motion picture camera, and in 1895 the Lumiere brothers made the first public motion picture presentation.

The Video Image

Early television monitors created images using a **cathode ray tube (CRT)**. In the tube a "gun" fires electrons at a phosphor-coated screen made up of small dots, or **pixels** (for *pic*ture *el*ements). When the electrons strike a pixel it glows. The more electrons that strike the pixel, the brighter it glows. This allows the television screen to recreate a pattern of bright and dark areas that look like highlights and shadows falling on objects and people. In a color monitor each pixel has a red, green and blue component. Red, green and blue are the **additive primary colors** of light. Adding these colors together in equal amounts creates white light. By adding different amounts of these colors together, any color in the visible spectrum can be recreated. In the CRT, by striking each color of the pixel with different amounts of electrons, the gun can create any color from the orange of a sunset to the purple of a plum to the skin color of a human being.

Unlike the film image in which the entire frame is seen at one time, the CRT does not create the image all at once. Each image is made up of hundreds of lines of pixels, and is drawn line by line. The electron gun scans the pixels in one horizontal line, then moves down to scan another line, and then another, and so on. The pattern of lines is called the **raster.**

In early television screens, by the time the gun had reached the bottom lines of the raster, the phosphor at the top of the screen had already begun to fade. Engineers solved this problem by using an

interlaced scan. In interlaced scanning the gun scans the first line, then skips to the third line, the fifth line and so on. It then returns to the top and scans lines 2, 4, 6 and all of the lines that it skipped over on the first scan. Each of these scans is referred to as a **field**, and the two fields together create a **frame**.

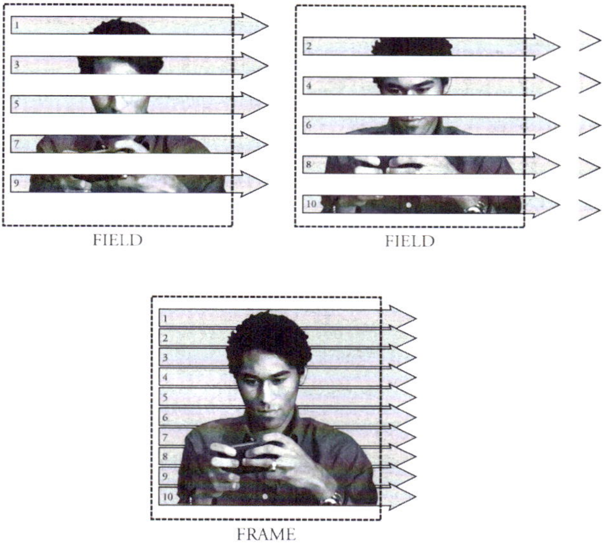

An interlaced frame. Each field consists of half of the lines that make up a video frame.

Film Styles

Today the terms "film" and "filmmaking" are commonly used to describe most motion pictures or movies, regardless of whether the work originated on film or digital video or is projected as a film or digitally projected.

Usually, any theatrically released motion picture is referred to as a "film." *Avatar* (2009) is regarded as a commercial film even though it was shot with digital cameras and digitally projected in most theaters. In general, cinematically constructed movies, short or feature length, are popularly referred to as films and will be referred to in that way throughout this book. Works in which the film or video technology is essential to the art form itself are usually more specifically identified.

Films are frequently categorized within one of four general styles: **narrative**, **documentary**, **animation** or **experimental**. Many films actually combine elements of two or more of these groups but can be described broadly by one of these terms.

The narrative film is probably the most recognizable type of film. Most theatrically released motion pictures fall into this group. Simply put, a narrative film tells a story. It is scripted and usually has a plot line with a beginning, middle and end, although the action may not unfold on screen in a linear fashion. The story may be presented in a simple straightforward way, as in John Ford's classic *Stagecoach* (1939) or in a more complex but still chronological way in a film like *Up in the Air* (2009), or the story might be presented in a very complex way, as in *Last Year at Marienbad* (1961) and *Memento* (2000). In the first examples the story unfolds in a linear, chronological order; in the second examples the action jumps backward and forward in time, and the viewer is forced to mentally create a chronology of events. In *Last Year at Marienbad* the filmmaker imposes the non-linear structure. In *Memento* the structure is motivated by the protagonist's memory loss, and the audience participates in his scattered experience of events. In any case a narrative film tells a story featuring characters whose actions advance the plot.

Documentaries are films that depict "real life." A documentary filmmaker uses the world around him, situations and people that actually exist, as source material. Among the very earliest filmmakers, France's Lumiere brothers began making documentaries in the 1890's. Their films presented everyday occurrences such as a train arriving at a station or workers leaving a factory at the end of the day. Over the decades filmmakers have documented events of global significance, such as wars and social upheavals, as well as smaller subjects such as ordinary individuals.

In its most basic sense a documentary is a film in which the filmmaker allows the action or events to unfold naturally with minimal interference. However, this definition breaks down the minute the filmmaker turns his camera from one subject to another or makes a cut. The very process involved in making a film requires that the artist manipulate the subject material to some extent. Differences in documentary style are often a matter of the degree of manipulation the filmmaker chooses to impose.

Documentary films can range from works like Robert Flaherty's *Nanook of the North* (1922), in which much of the action is actually staged, and Errol Morris' *The Thin Blue Line* (1988), in which some events are recreated using actors, to the "cinema verite" of Frederick Wiseman who, in works like *High School* (1968), manipulates his subjects in a subtler way through the editing structure he imposes on the footage. They can include lyrical, poetic films like the British documentary *Night Mail* (1936) and intimate personal histories like Werner Herzog's *Little Dieter Needs to Fly* (1998) and *Grizzly Man* (2005) as well as films dealing with historical events like Ken Burns' *Civil War* series (1990) and his World War II series, *The War* (2007). Some popular, theatrically released documentaries like Morgan Spurlock's *Super Size Me* (2004) and the films of Michael Moore seem to be conceived and constructed in support of a particular agenda. Davis Guggenheim's *Waiting For "Superman"* (2010) features the filmmaker traveling around the country, visiting schools and talking about his own kids' education. Frequently, the filmmaker is the subject of the "story," and some critics contend that these films should not be considered documentaries because they appear to promote a foregone conclusion. It should be noted that most documentaries promote opinions but in a less obvious way.

Animation is a type of filmmaking that creates the illusion of movement where none actually existed. Animators work with many different materials and with a wide variety of stylistic approaches. Drawings, objects, clay, puppets or other materials are manipulated in front of the camera. A single frame of film or a digital photograph is taken before replacing one piece of artwork with another that is slightly different or before moving the material or object into a slightly different position. Like a live action sequence, an animated sequence consists of a series of still images that each represents a progression from the previous one. If the increments of change are small enough and regular enough, a convincing illusion of motion will result. Classic drawn animation like *Pinocchio* (1940), clay animation like Nick Park's *Wallace and Gromit* films and eclectic works like Dave Borthwick's 1994 feature, *The Secret Adventures of Tom Thumb*, which combines clay animation with object animation and "pixilated" human actors, are a few examples of the variety found in traditional animation techniques and styles.

Technological breakthroughs in computer animation have made films like the *Toy Story* films (1995, 1999 and 2010) and Disney's 2009 release, *Up*, possible. Computer animation uses software that enables animators to digitally draw and build characters and environments. It has also become an integral element of live-action filmmaking. Movies like *Inception* (2010) and the 3-D release *Alice in Wonderland* (2010) are filled with computer animation that is composited with live-action elements.

Experimental filmmaking is the broadest and least easily defined category in terms of cinematic style. "Experimental" seems to be a catch-all term for any film that isn't a narrative or documentary. Often experimental films are not concerned with presenting a fictional story or documenting external reality. An experimental film might be more concerned with the graphic elements of the shots, with the play of light and shadow, color or movement. It might explore the technical limits of the filmmaking process itself: what happens when you edit together a series of single-frame shots or aim a video camera at a monitor displaying the image that the camera is shooting? Others might be interested in presenting a vision of internal reality, images from the filmmaker's subconscious.

Films that combine elements of narrative, documentary or animated filmmaking, films that blur the boundaries of the usual categories, are frequently classified as experimental films. In many cases these films reject traditional filmmaking techniques and values in favor of new, unusual approaches. Sometimes films that take an unconventional stylistic approach to narrative or documentary material are considered experimental. A few diverse examples of experimental films include Luis Bunuel's and Salvador Dali's surrealist short, *Un Chien Andalou* (1929), Maya Deren's 1943 psychodrama, *Meshes of the Afternoon*, Stan Brakhage's *Mothlight* (1963), which was made by putting bits of bugs and parts of plants onto a strand of clear film and fixing those artifacts onto the film with clear mylar tape (a "cameraless" film) and Martin Arnold's intricately detailed optical experiments, such as *Alone. Life Wastes Andy Hardy* (1998). Godfrey Reggio's *Koyaanisquatsi* (1983) and Jim Jarmusch's *Stranger than Paradise* (1984) are more widely known theatrical feature films that are usually considered experimental.

In the 1960s, with the advent of portable video cameras and recorders, artists began to create work that exploited the unique characteristics of the video format. This is called **video art** and, while it might seem similar to experimental film, it has distinct characteristics. These characteristics include the ability to record to tape and play back the footage almost instantly as well as the ability to record audio simultaneously. In addition, the electronic nature of video has enabled artists to explore new ways to manipulate imagery and sound with techniques like video feedback and the use of video mixers. In fact, video art is often concerned with manipulating the electronic signal itself.

Early video artists such as Nam June Paik worked with **single-channel video** as well as **video installation**. Single-channel video is displayed as a single image, projected or on a monitor. A video installation might involve multiple screens or the video may be part of an assemblage of various media. Advances in digital video technology have enabled contemporary video artists to work with a wide range of digital video editing and effects software. These new technological advances have also opened up the possibilities for interactive video art in which the viewer becomes a participant.

Chapter 2

The Film Camera and Film Stock

Film comes in many shapes and sizes. Small gauges of film have to be magnified to a greater degree in order to fill a movie screen, while larger gauges create a sharper, more detailed picture, since they require less magnification. There are film stocks that produce negative images and some that produce positive images, and film is manufactured with greater or lesser sensitivity to light.

The Photographic Image

At its most basic level motion picture film is a strip of flexible material made of **cellulose triacetate**. This celluloid **base** is thinly coated on one side with a chemical emulsion. The emulsion consists of light sensitive **grains** of silver compounds suspended in a gelatin. When the emulsion is exposed to light, a chemical reaction occurs. The grains that are exposed to light change their chemical structure. Those which are not exposed remain unchanged. At this point no image is visible on the film; it contains a **latent image**. In fact, if you were to look at the film immediately after exposure, it would not only look unchanged, but you would ruin your film because the emulsion is still light sensitive. In order to render the film insensitive to light and to make the latent image visible, the film must be **processed** in a chemical developer.

When a film stock is manufactured, the cellulose triacetate base material is coated with an emulsion of light sensitive silver compounds called silver halides. During exposure and processing some of these silver halides are converted into grains of metallic silver. Where more exposure takes place, more metallic silver is formed.

Each frame of a film consists of many tiny "dots" of grain, much like a pointillist painting. When the image is made up of more grains that are smaller, it appears smoother and more realistic. When the image is composed of fewer, larger grains, it appears rougher and more textured; the illusion of realism is lessened. Manufacturers make film in varying sensitivities. Large silver halide grains are more sensitive to light and are more easily exposed, while small grains are less sensitive and require a greater amount of exposure.

Film Formats

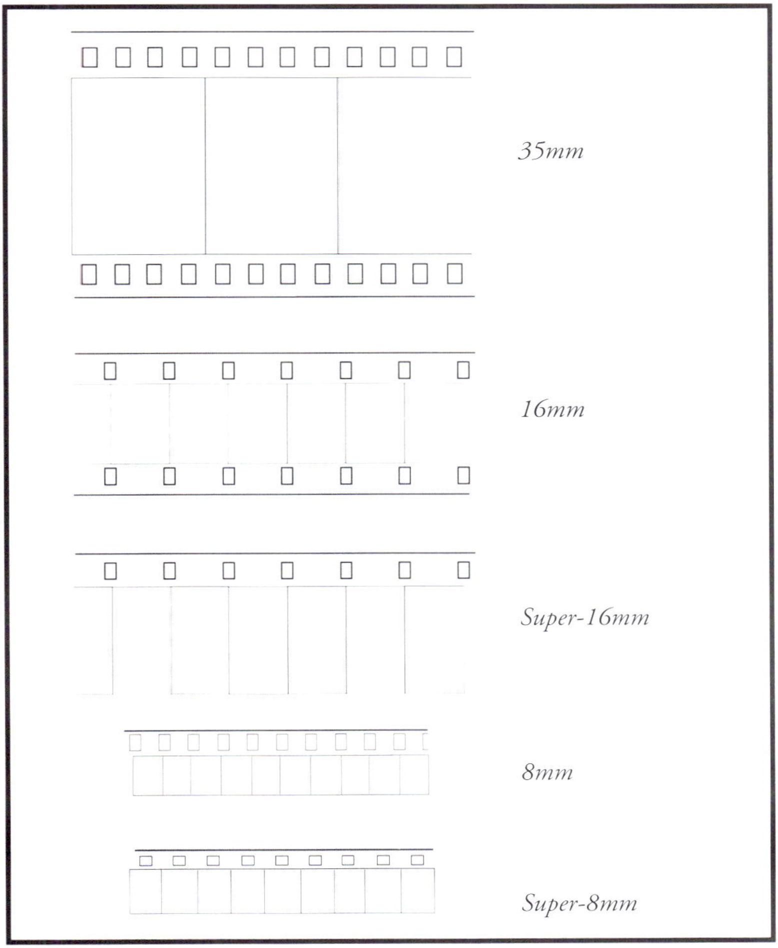

In filmmaking the term **format** refers to the gauge or width of the strip of film. The **35mm** format, the format used by Edison's first motion picture cameras, is still the standard today in feature and commercial filmmaking. 35mm film is 35 millimeters (about 1 1/2 inches) wide. Over the years other formats have been developed. In the 1920's the **16mm** format appeared as a less expensive alternative to 35mm. Originally aimed at home users, this format became useful to documentary filmmakers and newsreel photographers, because its smaller size meant a reduction in the size and weight of the motion picture camera used to expose it. The smaller camera improved the filmmaker's mobility and ability to shoot in confined spaces.

The **8mm** format came into existence in 1932. 8mm film was actually 16mm film with twice the number of sprocket holes. The 16mm film was run through an 8mm camera that exposed pictures along one edge of the film. After the entire roll of film passed through the camera, it was turned over, rethreaded and run through the camera again, exposing frames along the other edge. The processed film was then split down the middle lengthwise, resulting in two reels of 8mm film. In 1965 Eastman Kodak introduced **super-8mm** film. This format was the same width as regular 8mm, but the sprocket hole size was reduced and spacing was redesigned to provide a 50% larger frame, thereby greatly improving image quality.

There are larger film formats as well. Some big-budget epics are shot on 65mm film and released to theaters on the slightly wider 70mm format. Special venue formats, **Omnimax** and **Imax** are each shot on 65mm film, but in both cases a single frame is the size of three consecutive 65mm frames. These formats require enormously cumbersome and expensive cameras, but they can produce stunning images. Larger negatives contain more information (more grains of image) and can show greater detail on the screen.

The shape and relative dimensions of a frame of film in a given format are described by a simple numerical ratio of the frame's width to its height. This **aspect ratio** defines the shape of the rectangular frame. The motion picture frame is always a rectangle that is wider than it is high, but there can be some choice in the specific aspect ratio in some of the larger formats. Before 1953 almost all 35mm theatrical films had an aspect ratio of 1.33:1, meaning that the frame was one-and-one-third times wider than its height. This ratio can also be expressed as 4:3. If the projected image is four feet wide, it will be three feet high. Today, 35mm theatrical films are commonly shot with an aspect ratio of 1.85:1, a much wider rectangle, and some films are released to theaters with even wider aspect ratios, like 2.35:1. These wide-screen formats came about as the film industry sought new ways to attract audiences to theaters, a direct result of television's new popularity in the 1950s. 8mm, super-8mm and 16mm film all use the standard aspect ratio of 1.33:1 that was established in the early days of cinema.

The **super-16mm** format was introduced in the 1960's but was not widely used until the late 1980's. Super-16 uses standard 16mm film but the image is wider, resulting in an aspect ratio of 1.66:1. 16mm film is made with sprocket holes along both edges (**double-perf film**) or with sprocket holes along only one edge of the film (**single-perf film**). Standard 16mm films can be shot on either double-perf or single-perf film. Super-16 cameras simply shoot single-perf 16mm film in combination with a modified camera design that allows the wider image to fill most of the frame area on the film's other edge (where sprocket holes would exist on double-perf film). The film itself is not a different format from standard 16mm film.

Super-16mm is usually chosen when shooting a lower budget film that is intended for 35mm release. While the 16mm film and processing costs help keep the expenses down (when compared to 35mm), s-16 has an aspect ratio (1.66:1) that is much closer to the normal 35mm theatrical aspect ratio (1.85:1) than that of standard 16mm (1.33:1). Consequently, super-16 film can be **blown-up** (photographically enlarged from one format to another) to 35mm and the 1.85:1 aspect ratio with less magnification, and therefore with higher image quality. This also makes super-16 a good fit for video that uses a 16:9 aspect ratio. However, films shot in the s-16 format cannot be projected in the s-16 format. Since the image extends almost to the edge of the film, there is no room for a soundtrack. Super-16 films must be blown-up to 35mm or transferred to videotape or a digital format in order to be shown. Many theatrical feature films have been shot in the super-16 format, including Spike Lee's super-low budget *She's Gotta Have It* (1988), Darren Aranofsky's *The Wrestler* (2008) and Kathryn Bigelow's 2009 Oscar winner, *The Hurt Locker*, which was shot using a combination of s-16 and high definition video. Finally, it is worth noting that most European countries use a standard 35mm theatrical aspect ratio of 1.66:1, so s-16 can be blown-up perfectly for European release.

Camera Mechanics

The exposure of film in a movie camera is similar to that in still photography. In a motion picture camera the **shutter** opens and closes quickly, letting light hit the photosensitive material on the film to create a latent image. With the shutter closed the film is advanced; then the shutter opens again, exposing another frame. A movie camera captures the sequence of movement by exposing many separate frames each second.

Movie film comes rolled on the **feed reel**. As the camera's sprocket wheels turn, the teeth (or **sprockets**) engage the sprocket holes (or perforations) in the film, pulling it through the **camera gate**, the area behind the lens where the film is exposed to light. The sprocket wheels turn at a smooth, constant rate. But if the film went through the camera gate in constant motion the camera would not expose separate frames. Instead, each frame would be a blur. The film must not be moving when the shutter is open. The camera employs an **intermittent movement**, a stop-and-start movement, rather than constant motion to move the film through the gate. Since the

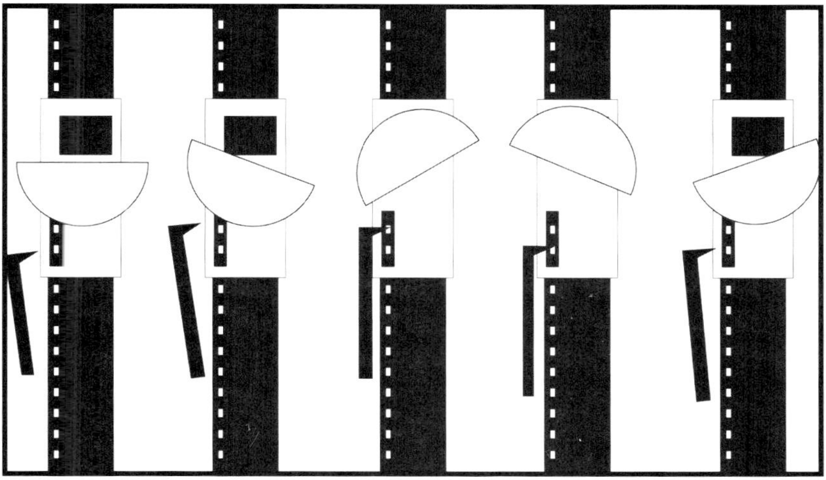

Intermittent movement. When the shutter is open the claw is disengaged and the film does not move. The claw moves up and engages a perforation. As the claw pulls the film down one frame, the shutter rotates so that it blocks the aperture and keeps light from hitting the film. As the shutter opening moves in front of the aperture, allowing light to hit the frame, the claw disengages and the film is again motionless.

sprocket drive moves constantly and the film in the gate does not, there must be some slack in the film between the sprocket wheels and the camera gate or the film will rip. This slack is formed by **loops** of film above and below the camera gate.

The camera gate consists of two plates. The **aperture plate** in front of the film has a rectangular opening, or aperture, through which light passes to strike the film. The rectangular aperture plate defines all four edges of the filmed image. The **pressure plate**, behind the film, presses on the film so that it remains flat against the aperture plate. Without the pressure plate the image would not stay in focus. In the gate the **pull-down claw** reaches up, engages a perforation and moves the film down one frame. The claw then disengages, reaching up for the next perforation. While the claw is disengaged the film is motionless, as light enters through the camera aperture and exposes a frame of the film. The pull-down claw completes this cycle many times each second, causing the film's intermittent movement through the gate. Many 16mm and 35mm cameras also employ a **registration pin**. The registration pin moves into a sprocket hole and holds the film absolutely still while the frame is being exposed.

If light were to hit the film all the time, the intermittent movement would not be effective. When the film moved it would blur the still frame just exposed. Light must be blocked from hitting the film while it is moving in order to prevent this. In a motion picture camera the shutter is a flat disc of metal that spins in front of the aperture plate. It spins in synchronization with the pull-down claw. While the claw is pulling the film down, the shutter shields the aperture and no light hits the moving film. While the pull-down claw is disengaged and the film is still, the **shutter opening** is in front of the aperture and the light exposes the film. The shutter is usually described by the size of its opening. A **180-degree shutter**, for instance, is a semicircle of metal. 180 degrees of the circle are metal, and the other 180 degrees are open, the shutter opening.

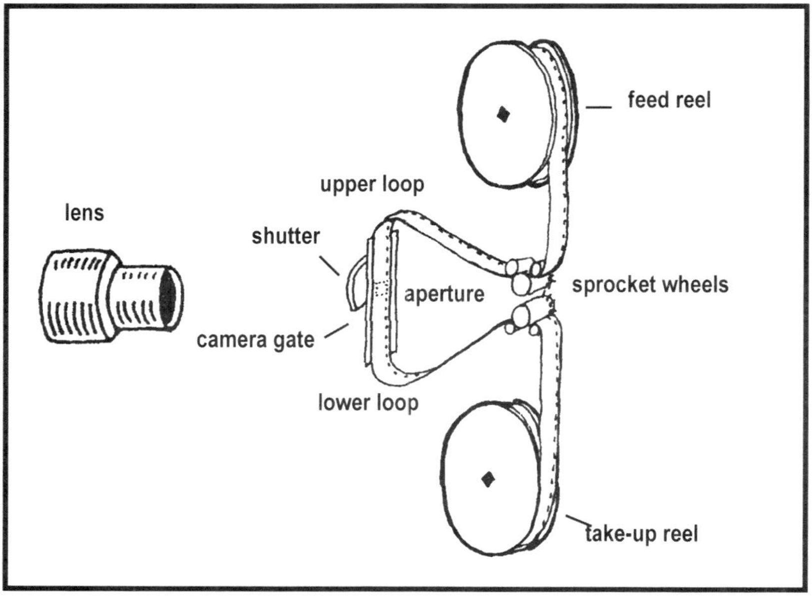

Diagram of a basic motion picture camera.

The film path in a movie camera starts at the feed reel. The film is routed to a sprocket wheel, and it forms an upper loop between the sprocket wheel and the camera gate. After passing through the gate the film forms the lower loop. Then it is engaged by another sprocket wheel that carries it to the **take-up reel**, where the film is wound and stored until it is developed. 16mm film is either packaged on a metal spool (100 feet of film wound onto a **daylight spool**), or it is wound in a 400-foot length on a plastic hub called a **core**. A daylight spool can be loaded into the camera in dim lighting. A core of film has no shielding and must be loaded in total darkness, either in a photographic darkroom or in a portable, light-tight **changing bag** or **changing tent**. In most cases 16mm film must be manually threaded through the camera. Super-8 film comes in a plastic cartridge, and everything behind the aperture plate (the reels, the sprocket drives, the loops, even the pressure plate) is inside the cartridge which is simply popped into the camera.

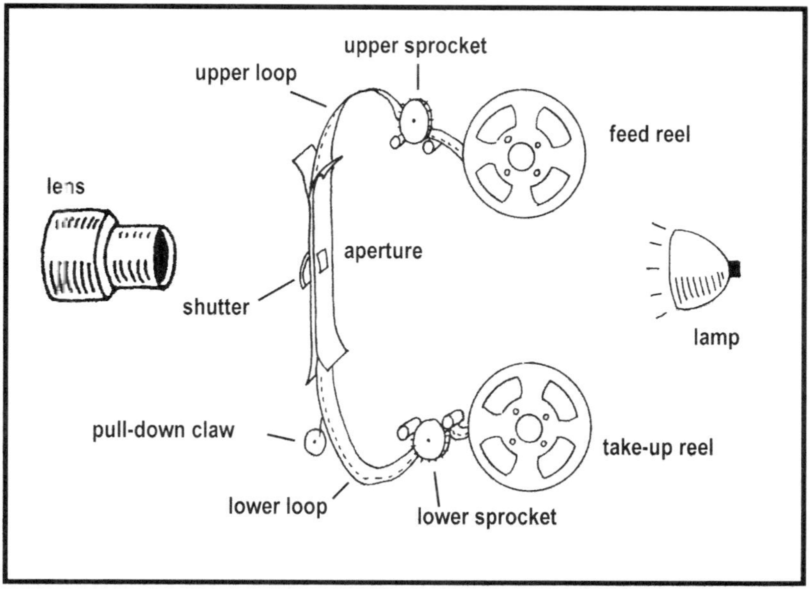

Diagram of a basic film projector.

Projected Motion

When the exposed film is later shown, it runs through a projector in much the same way it ran through the camera. The main difference is that instead of light entering the camera to expose the film, a powerful lamp throws light through the film as the projector's lens focuses the image onto a screen. In the projector, as in the camera, a shutter spins and blocks light while the film is moving so that only still images are seen.

Film moves through a camera at a steady rate, the **frame rate** (also called the **camera speed**), which is measured in frames per second (**fps**). "Sound speed," the standard for 16mm and 35mm film, is 24fps. Many super-8 cameras run at both 18fps and 24fps. Most of the time 18fps is used as the standard speed for super-8 film, but some filmmakers choose the 24fps standard when shooting super-8 for transfer to a digital format or with the intention of blowing it up to a larger film format. The speed of the camera by itself does not matter as much as the relationship between the frame rate of the camera and that of the projector. For motion to look natural on the screen *the projector must run at the same rate as the camera.* If the camera runs faster than the projector, then the result is slow motion. For instance, if the camera is run at 48fps, then an action that takes one second (e.g. lighting a match) will take up 48 frames of film. If the film is projected later at 24fps, those 48 frames will take two seconds to run through the projector. Everything will take twice as long as it did in real life.

Similarly, if the camera runs more slowly than the projection speed (**undercranking**), **fast motion** will result. For instance, if the camera runs at 12fps, that one-second match lighting will cover 12 frames of film. When run through a projector at 24fps, those 12 frames will go by in half a second; everything will move twice as fast as it did in real life. In **time lapse** photography the frame rate might be one frame per second, one frame every 10 seconds or as slow as a frame every minute or even every hour. Very slow frame rates produce extreme compression of time so that clouds might seem to whip through the sky or a flower can bloom in a few seconds.

Animation is a type of filmmaking that doesn't actually have a frame rate. Rather than speeding up or slowing down natural motion, an animator creates motion by manipulating materials in front of the camera while shooting single frames of film. For example, a drawn animated sequence showing pink elephants dancing might consist of 240 drawings of the elephants in positions that are each slightly different from the previous one. If one frame of each drawing is photographed, then the sequence will be 10 seconds long when projected at 24fps.

Negative and Reversal Film

a. b.

a) Negative film
b) Reversal film

Film stocks can be described as either **negative** or **reversal film**. During exposure and processing, some of the grains of silver halide in the emulsion are converted into grains of metallic silver. Where more exposure takes place, more metallic silver is formed. In negative film processing, the unexposed emulsion is converted to a waste product and washed away. Where a lot of light hit the film, a lot of metallic silver is left. Where no light hit the film, all of the emulsion is washed off; the negative film is clear in these areas. If run through a projector, light would shine through these clear areas, making a bright area on the screen. Where higher concentrations of metallic silver are left, less light would shine through the film. If enough light has exposed an area of the film, it will be practically opaque in that area. So with negative film, objects that were bright create a dark image, and dark objects create bright images. Brightness values on the film are the opposite of the way they appeared in the camera's viewfinder; a negative image is obtained. A filmmaker using negative film does not project the **camera original** film, the film that ran through the camera. To restore tonalities to their proper values, a **positive print** can be made from the negative. It is this positive print that is handled and projected.

THE NEGATIVE FILM PROCESS:

1. Silver halide grains are exposed to light.

2. Exposed grains are converted to silver.

3. Unexposed emulsion is washed away.

When reversal film is processed the emulsion that has reacted to light is first converted into grains of metallic silver, and then, in a processing step that is unique to reversal film, the metallic silver is bleached away. So, where a lot of light has hit the film, a lot of emulsion becomes metallic silver and is bleached away, and the film is clear. Where no light has hit the film a thick layer of unexposed emulsion is left. In reversal processing that remaining emulsion is re-exposed to light in the laboratory and then developed again, so that it becomes metallic silver. What was bright in front of the camera is bright on the screen. What was dark appears dark on the screen. The brightness and color values remain the same as what you saw through the camera. As a side effect, the emulsion that is left after developing is harder and more resistant to scratches than negative emulsion. It can therefore be run through a projector without being easily scratched.

THE REVERSAL FILM PROCESS:

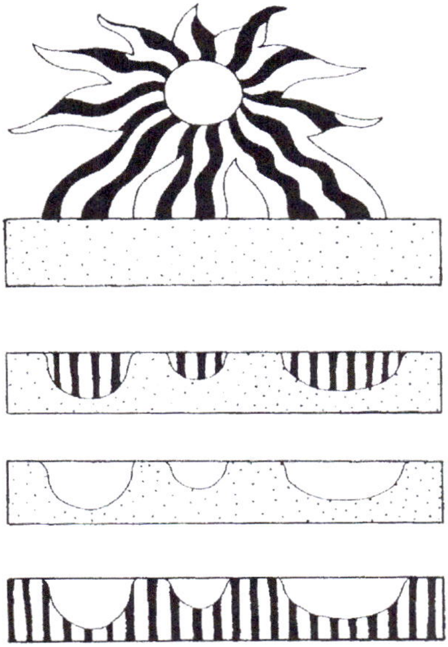

1. *Silver halide grains are exposed to light.*

2. *Exposed grains are converted to silver.*

3. *Silver grains are bleached away.*

4. *Remaining emulsion is re-exposed to light in the lab and developed a second time, resulting in a positive image.*

16mm film is available in both negative and reversal stocks. When 16mm negative is used as the camera original, the negative film is processed at the film laboratory and a print, known as a **workprint**, can be made from the negative. The workprint can be projected and edited by physically cutting and splicing it. It is much more common today, though, to make a positive videotape copy or a digital file from the negative and to edit this positive image in a digital editing program. The laboratory transfers (copies) the image from the camera original to video or directly to a digital file. The negative camera original is stored and under most circumstances is never handled at all. Sometimes, in the final stages of the editing process, the negative is carefully cut to match the workprint or the digital edit of the film. Then the edited negative can be used to make clean positive prints of the completed film. (For a more detailed discussion of the final stages of 16mm editing and printing, see Chapter 8, *Editing Mechanics*.)

Reversal film stocks are primarily intended (by the manufacturers) to be handled directly. That is, the camera original is processed at the film laboratory and it is projected and edited by the filmmaker. No print is involved. However, it is possible to make film prints or transfers (for digital editing or digital release) from reversal camera originals. While a few theatrical films, such as *Pi* (1998) and *Buffalo 66* (1998), have been shot on reversal film, the vast majority of professional filmmaking is done using negative film as the camera original. Reversal film has a different, generally harsher look than negative film. Negative film produces a much wider tonal range.

Super-8 film is available in both reversal and negative film. Filmmakers who are working in the super-8 format handle and edit their camera original film rather than having a print made, or else they have a transfer made and edit digitally. Often, the finished product is a video released on DVD, Blu-Ray or the web.

Black-and-White and Color

Another way to describe a film stock is by its color characteristics. With **black-and-white** (b&w) films only brightness values are reproduced. Black-and-white film stock does not react differently to different colors and does not reproduce color. If a red object reflects light as brightly as a green object, they will both appear as the same shade of gray on black-and-white film. The color film process involves the use of colored dyes. Color films react to and reproduce the colors of objects in the shot. The image on a strip of black-and-white film consists of varying densities of metallic silver. Many miniscule grains of metallic silver create the pattern that we see as the image on the screen. A color film image consists of varying densities of three different colored dyes. In color film processing the grains of metallic silver are replaced by tiny globs of cyan, yellow and magenta dye.

Film Sensitivity

Film stocks can also be described in terms of their sensitivity to light, or their **speed**. A **fast** film has grains that are larger and more sensitive to light. Less light is needed to cause them to react. **Slow** films have small, fine grains, and they require more light to achieve the same reaction. The speed of a film is expressed by an **EI** (Exposure Index) number. EI numbers are a way to compare the sensitivity to light of one film stock in relation to another. A film rated at EI 100 is twice as sensitive as a film rated at EI 50. It needs half as much light to achieve the same exposure. A film stock with a very high EI number is best to use under low lighting conditions. If there is plenty of light (outside on a sunny day, for instance) you might want to use a slower film, one with a lower EI number.

Note: EI numbers are the same as **ISO** (International Standards Organization) numbers and **ASA** (American Standards Association) numbers, and they can be used interchangeably with these other standards. They are *not* the same as **DIN** (Deutsche Industrie Norm) numbers, a European standard. While EI and ISO numbers have become the worldwide standards, people still commonly refer to ASA numbers as well, particularly in the United States.

A film is more sensitive to light if its light-sensitive grains are larger. When a film is projected onto a large screen, these grains are easy to see. Each grain is a tiny piece of the overall picture. An image made up of fewer large grains will not look as finely detailed as one that is made up of a larger number of small grains. That is one reason a filmmaker might want to use as slow a film as the light level will permit. Conventional thinking is that slow, fine-grained film stocks produce sharper, more realistic and therefore more believable pictures. They don't distract the audience by drawing attention to the surface of the medium or to the photographic process. Of course, there might be times when you want to do just that, so the choice of a film stock can be an aesthetic option as well as a practical one.

Any film stock needs a certain amount of light to achieve the correct exposure. If too much light hits the film, it will be **overexposed**; if too little light hits it, the film will be **underexposed**. If the film is overexposed too much, the film will not be able to handle the light and will begin to burn out and lose detail. In a greatly overexposed shot of the sky, for instance, the sky will be completely white. The blue color and the clouds will be washed out by too much light. If the film is *underexposed* too much, then again details get lost. In a severely underexposed shot of a man standing in the shadows, the film will show only a black mass where the shadow is. The man will be lost in the underexposed area.

The amount of overexposure and underexposure a film stock can handle without losing detail is called the **latitude** of the film. Reversal film has very limited latitude. If you underexpose or overexpose by even one stop, you will begin to lose detail in the darkest or brightest areas. Negative film has much wider latitude than reversal film and can handle a greater range of brightness values.

Color Balance

Using color film introduces an important point to the filmmaker: all light is not the same color. If you are reading this book outside in the sunlight, you see the sunlight reflecting off the page as white light. If you are inside reading by lamp light, you also see the light reflecting off the page as white light. This is because the eye and the brain, within certain boundaries, adjust to variations in the color of the light and see the dominant light as white (or neutral). In fact, daylight is much bluer than lamp light. You can see this easily when you are outside in the late afternoon and the lights have been turned on inside. The incandescent light shining through the windows of a house looks orange because your eyes are adjusted to the blue daylight. When you enter the house your eyes quickly adjust to the incandescent light and it appears white, without any color bias.

Although your eyes can adjust to variations in the color of light, film cannot. The color dyes in the light sensitive emulsion must be balanced during manufacturing to reproduce one, and only one, kind of light as white light. **Daylight-balanced** film reads daylight as white light. When using daylight-balanced film, uncorrected tungsten incandescent light will look orange. **Tungsten-balanced** film sees light from tungsten sources (such as movie lights or household light bulbs, but *not* fluorescent lights) as white light, and uncorrected daylight will look too blue. 16mm color film is available in both daylight-balanced and tungsten-balanced emulsions. When shooting daylight-balanced film under tungsten light, a blue **filter** (#80A filter) must be used to convert the orange tungsten light to the bluer color of daylight. When shooting tungsten-balanced film in daylight an orange filter (#85 filter) must be placed in front of the film. As the blue daylight passes through the filter, it is converted to the orange color of tungsten light. (Chapter 10, *Lighting*, includes a more in-depth discussion of color balance and light sources.)

Most super-8 cameras have a **filter switch** with two settings:  (a light bulb) and  (the sun). The filter switch controls the positioning of an orange #85 filter that is built into the super-8 camera. In the past, all of the available super-8 film stocks were balanced for tungsten light, and it was simply a matter of setting the switch to the proper icon. Today, there are both tungsten-balanced and daylight-balanced color films. Some are reversal and some are negative films. When shooting tungsten-balanced color film under tungsten lights, set the filter switch to the  position, and the orange #85 filter is *out*. It does not affect the light. When shooting this type of film with daylight as the light source set the switch to the  position and the filter is *in*, converting the blue daylight to the orange color of tungsten light. When shooting daylight-balanced film, always leave the switch in the  position with the orange #85 filter *out*. The color rendition will be correct when shooting in daylight. When shooting under tungsten light, the filter must still be in the *out* position, but it will be necessary to use a blue #80A filter in front of the lens in order to convert the orange tungsten light to the blue color of daylight.

When the filter is in it absorbs some of the light passing through it so that less light reaches the film. For this reason, when shooting black-and-white film, keep the filter out (the  position). Since black-and-white film does not react significantly to color variations anyway, there is no need for the filter and leaving it out allows the maximum amount of light to reach the film.

16mm cameras do not have filter switches. The light is filtered by mounting a glass filter in front of the lens. Some 16mm cameras (notably the Bolex) allow the filmmaker to insert a small gelatin filter behind the lens. In either case, the filter will absorb some of the light passing through it. To compensate for the lost light, tungsten-balanced films are rated as slower films (needing more light) when used in daylight with a #85 filter. The lower EI rating they are assigned simply factors in the light absorbed by the filter. (For a more detailed discussion of exposure, see Chapter 4, *The Lens*. For a more detailed discussion of color, see Chapter 10, *Lighting*.)

Black-and-white films have a nominally lower EI rating under tungsten light than they have under daylight. This is because black-and-white films are slightly more sensitive to blue light than to other parts of the spectrum, and daylight contains an abundance of blue light. No filtration is necessary when shooting black-and-white film, regardless of the type of light illuminating the subject.

Film Stocks

16mm film is available in a variety of lengths. A 100-foot roll of 16mm film has a running time of two minutes and 47 seconds at 24fps. A 400-foot roll will run for eleven minutes and eight seconds at 24fps. There are 40 frames in one foot of 16mm film.

All super-8 films are packaged in light-tight plastic cartridges containing 50 feet of film. The running time of a cartridge is three minutes and 20 seconds at 18fps (or two minutes and 30 seconds at 24fps). There are 72 frames in one foot of super-8 film, so at 18fps it takes four seconds for one foot to move through the camera.

The specific film stocks available to users change regularly, and improvements in emulsion technology are on-going. For a complete listing of the motion picture film stocks that are currently available from Eastman Kodak, check online at *www.kodak.com/go/motion*.

Chapter 3

The Video Camera and Recorder

In a video camera a lens collects light rays and focuses them onto a video chip called a **charge-coupled device** (**CCD**). The CCD changes light values into electrical voltage. The brighter the light hitting the CCD, the stronger the voltage. The CCD is made up of thousands of pixels. Light striking a pixel causes a build-up of electrical charge. In the time that one video frame is taken, the pattern of light and shadow causes different charges to build up on each of the thousands of pixels on the CCD. For instance, if the camera is framing a bright object centered against a dark background, then the pixels in the center of the CCD will have a very strong charge and the pixels around them will have a weak charge. The portion of the signal corresponding to the center pixels would have a higher voltage than the portion of the signal corresponding to the edges. This occurs frame after frame as long as the camera is on and light strikes the CCD. When the voltage signal from the CCD is read by a monitor, the higher voltage creates a bright area on the screen and lower voltage creates areas of darkness.

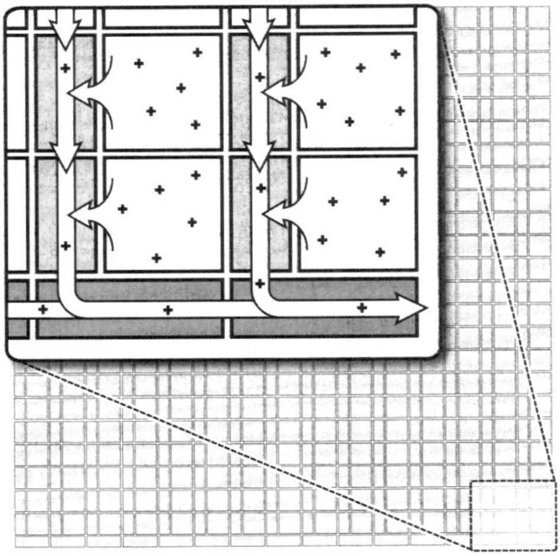

A charge-coupled device (CCD). Individual pixels build up an electrical charge when exposed to light. The charges move out of the CCD to create a continuous voltage signal.

Three-CCD cameras (also called **three-chip cameras**) use a prism to break the incoming light into separate red, green and blue portions, each of which is recorded by a separate CCD. These cameras create sharper images and more accurate colors than **one-chip** cameras. In addition, a bigger CCD with more pixels will generally render better images that a smaller CCD. CCD sizes are usually given in inches (a measure of the diagonal size of the chip) or megapixels (thousands of picture elements).

Video Formats

Early video signals created only brightness differences; a pixel could be black, white or any shade of gray in between. This black-and-white video played at 30 frames per second in the United States. Each frame was made up of two interlaced fields (see Chapter 1, *The Moving Image*). When color TV was developed, in order to add color information and create full-color video that would be compatible with older black-and-white televisions, engineers had to slow the speed down by one tenth of one percent to 29.97 fps, the current speed of **standard-definition** video in the United States. This standard, 29.97 interlaced frames per second was set by the **National Television System Committee** and is referred to as **NTSC** video, or standard-definition (**SD**) video.

NTSC video uses an aspect ratio of 4:3. Since an NTSC frame is 480 lines high, it seems that each line should be 640 pixels wide to create the proper 4:3 ratio. This would be true, however, only if the pixels themselves were square. Since SD video pixels are actually rectangles that are higher than they are wide, it takes 720 of these pixels to create an image of the correct aspect ratio. Therefore, a full-size NTSC video frame measures 720 x 480 pixels, meaning that it consists of 480 horizontal lines that are each 720 pixels wide.

Standard-definition video has largely been replaced by **high-definition** (**HD**) video formats. High-definition video features frames with at least 720 horizontal lines. This is much more than NTSC's 480 lines and results in a cleaner, more detailed image. In addition, HD has a 16:9 "widescreen" aspect ratio, making the HD image much larger than the SD image. HD formats use square pixels rather than NTSC's rectangular pixels.

There are currently three HD formats: **720p** uses 720 lines of 1280 pixels each (1280x720) in a **progressive** frame. A progressive frame is not divided into fields like an interlaced frame. All the horizontal lines are displayed at once. **1080i** uses a more detailed, 1920x1080 interlaced frame. Much of the greater detail in the 1080-line frame, though, is cancelled out by interlacing, so many HD devices also show **1080p**, which uses a 1920x1080 pixel progressive frame.

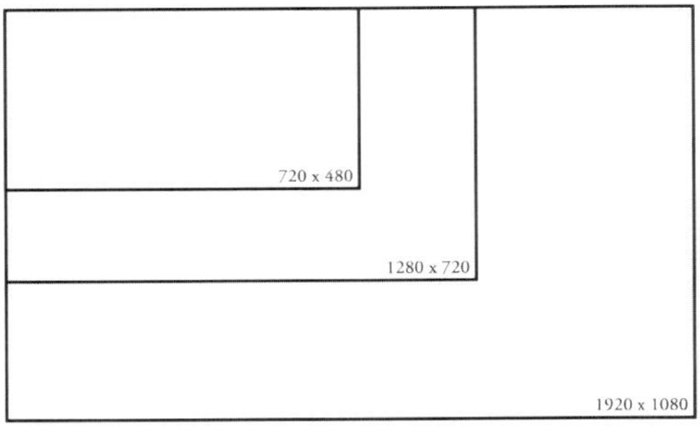

Relative sizes of video frames.

Video Exposure

The range from the darkest image that can be recorded to the brightest that can be handled is called the **contrast range**. The human eye has a very large contrast range; a person can simultaneously see detail in deep shadow and also in sunshine hundreds of times brighter. The brightest light that a video camera can handle may be only 40 times brighter than the darkest. The contrast range would be expressed as 40:1. This means that to make a scene look natural and pleasing on video, light must be carefully controlled so that all brightness values fall within this very limited range.

If too much light strikes a pixel, a charge builds up that is the maximum the pixel can hold. This causes a loss of detail in this part of the video frame. A bright window, for example, may be shown as a featureless white rectangle on video, though the human eye may see trees and buildings outside the window. If too little light hits a pixel the charge may be too weak to be picked up as part of the video signal, again causing a loss of detail. A person standing in deep shadow may be visible to the human eye, but the shadow will be rendered in the video signal as featureless black and the person will not be seen.

If there is little light striking the CCD, the video signal will be very weak and the image will be dark. This image can be made brighter by amplifying the strength, or **gain**, of the voltage. Making an image brighter by boosting the gain can result in an inferior image, because there are stray charges floating through any electrical system. Normally these stray charges are so small that they do not affect the video signal or the resulting image. If the signal is amplified, however, these slight charges can become strong enough to show up as "light" on the video image. These areas of random brightness are referred to as **video noise**. The more the signal is amplified, the noisier the image becomes. For this reason, it is better to adjust exposure using the lens (see Chapter 4, *The Lens*) than by adjusting video gain.

Video cameras use shutter speed to control how long light strikes the CCD pixels. Some cameras use a mechanical shutter, a disc that spins in front of the CCD prism similar to the shutter of a film camera (see Chapter 2, *The Film Camera and Film Stock*). Most inexpensive cameras use an electronic shutter, which turns the CCD on for a fraction of a second and then deactivates it before turning it on again. The length of time that the CCD is activated is the shutter speed, since that is the only time that the pixels convert light into an electrical charge.

There are many shutter speeds available for use, from as long as 1/24 sec to as fast as 1/10,000 sec. A faster shutter speed means that light will strike the active CCD for a shorter period of time. Therefore, less of the available light is converted to voltage, and the image is darker. Very fast shutter speeds usually cannot be used in low-light situations. A very slow shutter speed, however, will mean that if an object or person moves, the light reflecting from it will cover several pixels while the image is being recorded, causing **motion blur**. Too much motion blur can be distracting, but many people feel that too little makes a video image look unrealistically "sharp." For instance, when shooting a circular fan, the whirling blades may appear as a blur to both the human eye and to the video camera when shot at slower shutter speeds. At faster shutter speeds each individual fan blade may be clearly visible on the video; in each frame the new position of the blades will be clearly defined so that the fan blades appear to "skip" unnaturally to a new place in each frame.

White Balance

The **white balance** of a camera adjusts the sensitivity of the red, green and blue color components to change the overall color of the image. This is necessary because light from different sources can have very different color qualities. White balancing the camera so that the primary light is seen as white can be done in one of several ways. On some cameras the white balance controls will be accessible in the menu settings. In others, the camera will have a white balance button or dial, but nearly all cameras will have the same options available, and the process of setting the white balance will be very similar.

Automatic white balance lets the camera read the color of the primary light and adjust the sensitivity of the red, green and blue components of the CCD so that the light appears white. If the light changes, the camera may re-balance in the middle of a shot, causing all the colors in the frame to change suddenly.

Manual white balancing is preferable to automatic balancing and can be done one of two ways: by adjusting to the light actually present, or by setting the camera to a standard white balance and making the light sources match this setting. White balance "presets" can read either tungsten light or daylight as white light. (For a more detailed discussion of color see Chapter 10, *Lighting*.)

To manually set the white balance of the camera, hold a white card in front of the camera and zoom in so that it fills the frame. The white card should be held under the light that the subject is to be shot under. You then set the white balance by pressing a button or switch on the camera and holding it until a display in the viewfinder indicates that the white balance has been set. The CCD(s) are now adjusted so that the light that is striking the card will show as white on the video. If another source of light in the frame gives off light of a different color temperature, that light will be seen as colored light on the video.

Suppose an actor is shown in a room lit by tungsten light, but a bathroom lit by fluorescent lights and a window letting daylight into the room are visible in the frame. If the tungsten light is used for white balance the actor will look natural, but the fluorescent light will make the bathroom look green, and the light coming in the window will appear blue. If, in the next shot, the fluorescent light is used for illumination (because the actor is now in the bathroom), then the camera should be manually white balanced again with the white card held under the fluorescent light. Now the actor will look natural under the fluorescent light, and the tungsten light in the main room will look yellow. The color of the daylight will also change to a different shade of blue. For this reason, it is usually better to control the lighting so that all light sources give off light of the same color.

Since focus, exposure, color and other features of the image will be judged by looking at the viewfinder or a monitor, it is important that the viewfinder and monitor are adjusted so that they are giving correct information. If the viewfinder brightness has been turned down, for instance, making the image look bright enough on the viewfinder may result in overexposing the image on video. Before shooting, the brightness and contrast controls for the viewfinder should be checked, and they should be adjusted if necessary.

Some viewfinders will display **zebra stripes**, a pattern of diagonal stripes that appear on any areas of the frame that exceed a certain brightness level. This helps to avoid overexposing portions of the frame. In some cameras, the level at which zebra stripes are displayed is factory set and cannot be changed. In others the zebra stripe level can be set manually. The zebra stripes are visible only in the viewfinder and are not recorded.

Many digital cameras have a fold-out LCD screen. The image on an LCD screen looks different when viewed from different angles. During shooting, always try to maintain the proper angle in relation to the LCD screen so that you are seeing the image accurately. The viewfinder will often give a much more accurate rendition of the brightness and contrast of the image being recorded.

A video camera with LCD screen.

The CCD and the lens are the features of a camera that most directly affect the quality of the image, and the controls affecting them are the most important tools for creating the desired look of the video. Most cameras have a variety of other controls that are usually adjusted using a **menu**, text displayed in the viewfinder that shows the various controls, the options for each control and the option currently selected for each one. Most cameras, except for the most expensive ones meant only for professional use, have modes of operation in which most menu settings are preset. For example, in "sports" mode the shutter speed might be preset to a very fast setting in order to minimize motion blur, and the white balance would likely be set to daylight. There is also an "automatic" mode in which focus, exposure, white balance and all main controls automatically change to reflect changing shooting conditions, unless the filmmaker locks these settings.

The less expensive a camera is, the more likely it is to rely on automatic controls, and the less likely it is that these controls will actually give satisfactory results. You should take time before every shooting session to make sure that all menu options are set to the desired settings and make necessary adjustments consciously rather than relying on the machine to make them. This is especially true if more than one person uses the camera, if it has been borrowed from a friend or if it is a school camera checked out by multiple users. In these cases nothing can be taken for granted. The previous user may have set a menu option in such a way as to unwittingly sabotage your shoot. If you are careful and check the menu settings thoroughly before shooting, this can be avoided. You should familiarize yourself with all of the camera controls and menu functions so that they can be found and manipulated quickly under pressure during a shoot.

The Video Recorder

As light reflects from people or objects moving in front of the camera, the fleeting patterns of light, shadow and color are turned into the pattern of continuously varying voltage created by the camera's CCD. This voltage pattern must be recorded so that it can be played back at a later date. Originally, this was the function of the **videotape recorder** (**VTR**). A VTR that is a separate piece of machinery from the camera is often referred to as a **video deck** or simply as a "deck." It is common for a camera and recorder to be combined into one unit, a **camcorder**.

In the **record head** of the VTR or camcorder, the voltage pattern produced by the CCD is converted into a pattern of changing magnetic charges. These changing magnetic charges must be recorded onto some magnetically sensitive material. **Videotape** is a flexible material that is coated on one side with **oxide**. The oxide contains tiny particles of metal. When these are exposed to a magnetic charge the particles pick up the charge, becoming tiny magnets themselves. If they are not exposed to another magnetic field, they will hold the charge.

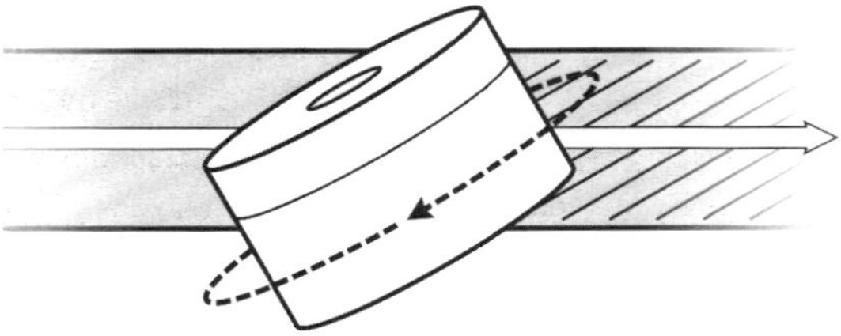

The head drum of a videotape recorder showing the helical scan.

These magnetic charges are laid onto the tape as it is wrap-ped around the **head drum**, a cylindrical rotating drum that contains multiple record heads. As the tape passes, it winds around the drum diagonally. As the drum rotates, the heads create a diagonal path of magnetized particles called a **helical scan**. The heads typically include not only the record heads but also **erase heads** that remove any pre-existing magnetic signal that may be on the tape. This makes it easier for the record heads to lay down a new magnetic signal. The heads also include **playback heads** which read the magnetic charges on the tape. When the recorded videotape is run past the heads, they read the charges that have been recorded onto the tape. In an analog system, these charges are turned directly back into a continuously changing voltage signal that is fed to the monitor to create the video image. Since this voltage signal is a direct analog of the magnetic charges on the tape, and those charges are a direct analog of the signal from the CCD, this type of recording is referred to as **analog** recording.

There are two problems with analog recording. The first is that any problem affecting the pattern of magnetic charges will affect the resulting image. For instance, stray magnetic charges affect particles of the material and may cause "noise" on the image. The second is that every time analog material is copied, or **dubbed**, more noise is introduced into the image, and the image is degraded with every new dub. This is known as **generational loss**. The original magnetic pattern is called the "first generation" recording. A copy of the original is the second generation. A copy made from that copy is the third generation. Every generation that an image goes through causes further generational loss and an increasingly degraded image.

Modern video recorders use **digital** recording methods which convert the video signal into a series of numbers. The **binary** number system is one in which any number is made up of a string of digits, and each digit can have one of only two values: 0 or 1. The voltage values of a video signal are converted to binary numbers which can then be recorded as magnetic charges in the VTR. This is done in the recorder's **analog-to-digital converter** (**A-D converter**). When the video is played back, the machine reads the numbers and its **digital-to-analog converter** (**D-A converter**) converts them back to the proper voltage values needed to create the image on the monitor. Since the machine only has to reproduce the correct numbers, noise or imperfections in recording do not matter. It makes no difference if a "1" is recorded clearly or noisily, as long as the machine reads it as a "1" and not a "0." For this reason digital signals are usually much clearer than analog ones. Also, reproducing the correct numbers will result in the exact same signal no matter how many copies are made; there is no generational loss. Digital copies made by copying digital data from one machine to another are called **clones** rather than dubs, and a clone will be exactly the same as the original.

There are two characteristics that determine how accurately the digital information will reproduce the video signal. The first is the **sampling rate**. As the signal is fed into the A-D converter, it checks, or samples, the signal many times and converts the voltage information into a binary number. The sampling rate is the measure of how many times the information is sampled, expressed in **kilohertz** (**kHz**), thousands of times per second, or **megahertz** (**MHz**), millions of times per second. The higher the sampling rate, the more information is gathered, and the more accurately the voltage signal is reproduced.

Equally important is the **bit rate** or **bit depth** of the samples. The bit rate states how many digits, or **bits**, will describe each sample. A higher bit rate means that more information can be recorded, making the image more detailed and accurate. In most digital video systems the red, green and blue information is written in separate 8-bit strings, for a total of 24 bits.

Some digital cameras, instead of using a CCD and an A-D converter, use a similar chip called a **Complementary Metal Oxide Semiconductor** (**CMOS**) chip. A CMOS chip converts light into voltage in a similar way to a CCD, but the digital processing is performed by the chip itself. CCDs and CMOS chips are often referred to as image sensors.

In a digital VTR the 1s and 0s created by the CMOS or the A-D converter are laid down to magnetic tape in the same way as the voltage signal in analog recorders. In analog recorders the system of magnetic heads and magnetically sensitive videotape was the only option. Though many digital camcorders still use videotape, most now record to solid-state data cards like Compact Flash, Secure Digital or Panasonic's P2 cards. Others record to portable hard drives that store the video information on spinning magnetic disks just as a computer stores data, or to optical discs like DVDs. In these recorders the complex system of record heads and helical scanning is replaced with a process where 1s and 0s from the A-D converter are simply stored as data, making it easier to transfer the information to an editing system.

Video Compression

Because a video signal consists of huge amounts of information, most digital recorders use **compression** to make the video signal smaller by removing some of the information. In order to be seen correctly the signal must undergo **decompression** on playback. The series of algorithms that control *co*mpression and *dec*ompression are referred to as a **codec**.

Different video codecs compress the video in different ways. Some use **temporal compression**, which actually discards some of the frames of video on compression and then creates "predicted frames" to replace them on decompression. Temporal compression is typically applied after editing to make video easier to distribute. More common in video recorders is **spatial compression**, which keeps all of the frames but removes some information from each frame.

Video Signals

To get the video signal from one place (such as the VTR) to another (such as a monitor) special cables and connectors must be used. A **composite** video signal combines the **luminance**, or brightness information, with the **chrominance**, or color information. This combined signal is sent through a cable with a single connection. Combining all of this information into a single signal results in a relatively low-quality image, and composite connections are usually not used in professional video equipment.

An **S-video** cable has several pins that carry the luminance and chrominance information separately. Since luminance is usually represented by the letter "Y" and chrominance by the letter "C," an S-video connection is sometimes referred to as a **Y-C** connection. Splitting the signal into two parts allows for higher image quality.

A **component** video signal not only separates luminance from chrominance, but breaks the chrominance information into two signals as well, meaning that a component signal must be carried over three cables. To save a cable (as well as bandwidth) the green color component is left out, since it can easily be obtained by subtracting the red and blue components from the luminance information. For this reason, the three components of a component video signal are usually designated Y, R-Y and B-Y.

Many digital devices move video to a monitor or projector by converting it to an analog signal and sending it along a component or composite connection. This results in a severe loss of quality. To allow the signal to remain digital, and therefore higher quality, most devices use an **HDMI** (**High-Definition Multimedia Interface**) connection. An HDMI cable can carry an uncompressed, high quality video signal that is compatible with many different devices and codecs along with several audio channels.

Chapter 4

The Lens

Strictly speaking, the lens is not part of the camera. As the "pin-hole" camera demonstrates, a lens is not necessary to expose film. A pin-hole camera consists of a light-tight box with a tiny hole in one side that allows light to enter the box. Light entering through the pin hole exposes film on the opposite side of the box. However, it takes several seconds for this small amount of light to expose the film. The basic function of a lens is to gather and focus light rays more efficiently. A camera lens consists of several pieces of glass, or **elements**, arranged inside a tube called the lens barrel.

Focal Length

A lens is referred to by its **focal length**, which is determined by the arrangement of lens elements within the lens barrel. Focal length is an expression of the lens' size, usually stated in millimeters (mm). The focal length determines a lens' degree of image magnification. Lenses of different focal lengths will reproduce the same shot in different ways. A "normal" lens reproduces an image as closely as possible to the way the human eye sees it, with the least distortion of perspective. In the 16mm format a 25mm lens is considered normal. In super-8 a normal lens is one with a focal length between 12mm and 15mm. A 50mm lens is considered normal in the 35mm format. In a video camera, the smaller the chip the shorter the focal length that is considered normal. Some video cameras use chips that have approximately the same dimensions as a 35mm film frame so that they can use the same lenses that are used on 35mm film cameras.

A lens with a shorter focal length (under 25mm on a 16mm camera, less than 12mm in super-8) will gather light rays from a wider angle of view in front of it, and therefore it is called a **wide-angle lens**. Because of its short focal length a wide-angle lens can also

Three shots from the same distance and camera position with different lenses. Top, wide-angle lens; middle, normal lens; bottom, telephoto lens.

be referred to as a **short lens**. These lenses tend to exaggerate the depth of a shot. An object will seem to be farther from the back wall than it is in reality. A woman walking toward the camera will appear to be moving faster than she is in reality, because her image will grow in size very quickly as she nears the camera. Wide-angle lenses can also cause horizontal lines to bend. The horizon line in a landscape, for instance, may curve slightly at either end of the frame. At very short focal lengths both of these effects are exaggerated, and the image becomes excessively curved and distorted. An extreme wide-angle lens that causes such effects is known as a **fisheye lens**.

A **long lens**, or **telephoto lens** (over 25mm on a 16mm camera, over 15mm in super-8), accepts light rays from a narrower angle of view in front of it. Small details of the scene will fill the frame. For instance, in three shots of a person from a fixed camera position, a wide-angle lens might show the person and some of the background. A normal lens might show the person from the waist up. A telephoto lens might show just the person's face. Since the telephoto lens seems to magnify small details of the scene, any unsteadiness of the camera will also be magnified so that a handheld or dolly shot using a long lens may be unacceptably shaky. If image steadiness is a concern, use a wide-angle lens. When using a telephoto lens, use a tripod. In addition, long lenses introduce some distortion. In contrast to wide-angle lenses which increase the perceived depth of a shot, telephoto lenses make the shot seem flatter. An actor in front of a wall will seem to be right up against it, even though he might be standing a considerable distance away from it.

This discussion has treated lenses as prime lenses. A **prime lens** has only one fixed focal length. A 10mm lens is only a 10mm lens, and a 75mm lens is only a 75mm lens. Prime lenses, or fixed focal length lenses, are frequently used in 16mm and 35mm filmmaking. Most of the cameras used in these formats accept a variety of lenses, and lenses can be changed quickly and easily. It is common practice to use different prime lenses for different shots and situations.

The same 25mm lens, used on three different cameras shooting three different film formats, would have very different magnification effects. On a 16mm camera, it would be a normal lens; on a super-8 camera it would be a telephoto lens; and it would be a wide-angle when mounted on a 35mm camera. That is due to the fact that a lens' focal length is relative to the size of the frame onto which it focuses light. The same relationship is true with video cameras and digital cameras that have an electronic image sensor instead of film. The magnification effects of a given lens are relative to the size of the image sensor.

Frequently, it is more convenient to use a variable focal length lens, a **zoom lens**, rather than prime lenses. Zoom lenses have a continuous range of focal lengths, from wide angle to telephoto. They are usually referred to by the range of focal lengths they cover. A "12-to-120 zoom" can be used as a 12mm wide-angle lens, a 120mm telephoto lens or at any focal length in between. With prime lenses, in order to change the composition from a long shot to a close-up, it is necessary to either move the camera or remove the lens and replace it with another. Using a zoom lens it is possible to zoom in to a telephoto shot or zoom out to a wide-angle shot by just turning a dial.

If you change focal lengths while the camera is running the result is a "zoom" shot. Before you use the zoom effect in a shot, as with any other camera movement, ask yourself why you want to do it. Is there a legitimate reason? Is the zoom appropriate or are you just bored? Zooms, like dollies, pans or tilts, should be designed to add or reveal important information within a shot. Zooming that is not motivated can be distracting and can look sloppy.

In 16mm, 35mm and high-end video cameras zoom lenses are typically used in conjunction with prime lenses. Almost all super-8 cameras and most low-end video cameras include a built-in zoom lens that cannot be removed. Sometimes these cameras do not specify focal lengths in millimeters, but as a continuum from "W" (wide angle) to "T" (telephoto). Most video cameras also have an electronic motor that can control the speed of zooming.

Some lenses are **macro lenses**. Since many lenses cannot focus on anything closer than four feet away, a special lens is needed to shoot extreme close-up shots. A macro lens can focus on objects as near as several inches in front of the lens. While individual macro lenses used in 16mm, 35mm and high end video simply allow the filmmaker to focus closer by turning the lens' focusing ring, super-8 cameras and video camera lenses may require the filmmaker to flip a switch on the camera body or the lens in order to change the camera from its normal focusing range to the macro focusing range. If you want to fill the frame with a postage stamp or show a cricket on a stalk of grass, use a macro lens.

Film Exposure

In addition to gathering and focusing rays of light, lenses are used to control the amount of light reaching the film. When you enter a dark room on a sunny day, you can't see anything at first. Slowly your eyes adjust to the low light level and you can see details. The eye adapts to varying amounts of light by opening or closing its iris to let the right amount of light reach the retina.

A camera lens also has an iris, a metal diaphragm that can be opened or closed to control the amount of light reaching the film. If too much light hits the film, it will be overexposed. If too little light hits the film, it will be underexposed. The right amount of light is determined by the speed (sensitivity to light) of the film. A *fast* film is more sensitive and needs less light than a slow film. (Film speed and the numerical rating systems that define it are discussed in detail in Chapter 2, *The Film Camera and Film Stock.*)

Whatever the speed of the film, it always needs a specific combination of exposure time and amount of light to be correctly exposed. The film's exposure time, or **shutter speed**, can only be controlled by changing the camera's **shutter angle** (simply another term for shutter opening) or by changing its running speed (fps). Most motion picture cameras don't provide the user with a way to change the shutter angle, and changing a camera's running speed to control exposure time is rarely an option, since a change in the frame rate also results in a change in the speed of motion on the screen.

As discussed earlier (in Chapter 2, *The Film Camera and Film Stock*), the shutter of a motion picture camera rotates in front of the aperture plate, alternately letting light expose the film and then blocking light out. The shutter speed is the actual length of time that the shutter lets light expose each frame of film. In order to increase the exposure time on the film, the shutter opening must be in front of the film for a longer period of time, and therefore the shutter must spin more slowly. Since the shutter of a motion picture camera is synchronized to the camera's intermittent drive, the only way to slow the shutter down is to slow down the camera's frame rate. For instance, at 12fps the shutter will let light hit the film twice as long as it would at 24fps. However, shooting at 12fps will result in fast motion. So, while manipulation of the shutter speed might be a viable means of controlling exposure for a still photographer who shoots one picture at a time, for the filmmaker changing the shutter speed is seldom a practical way to control the exposure of the film.

The amount of light hitting each frame of the film can be controlled in two ways: by actually changing the amount of light in the scene or by opening or closing the lens iris. If you are shooting outside on a sunny day, it's hard to change the amount of light in the scene. Often you'll have to use the available light (controlling light is discussed in detail in Chapter 10, *Lighting*). In most cases the best way to control the amount of light that hits the film is by opening or closing the iris in the lens. Just as the shutter speed determines *how long* light will hit each frame, the size of the iris opening will determine *how much* light hits the frame. (Note: the iris opening is also referred to as the lens **aperture**. Do not confuse this *adjustable* aperture in the lens with the fixed, rectangular camera aperture in the camera gate which is simply a frame-sized window cut into the aperture plate.)

An **f-stop** is a number that indicates the size of the circular opening of the lens aperture (or iris). Every serious filmmaker should know the f-stop series:

1 1.4 2 2.8 4 5.6 8 11 16 22 32 45

← *"opening up"* *"stopping down"* →

As the f-stop numbers get higher, the size of the lens aperture opening is actually getting smaller, letting less light in. As the f-stop numbers get lower the aperture opening gets larger, letting more light in. Every time you **open up** one **stop** (from f/4 to f/2.8, for instance) you *double* the amount of light reaching the film, because you *double* the area of the lens' circular opening. When you **stop down** one stop (from f/4 to f/5.6, for instance) you let *half* as much light in. If you change by more than one stop, every stop doubles or halves the light. For example, if you open up 3 stops (from f/4 to f/1.4, for instance), then you double the light 3 times to let in 2 x 2 x 2 = 8 times as much light. The list of f-stop numbers above is not exhaustive but a filmmaker will rarely, if ever, deal with lens openings larger than f/1 or smaller than f/45.

Video Exposure

If too much light strikes a pixel, a charge builds up which is too strong for the pixel to hold, and some of the charge will "spill" out onto nearby pixels. This causes a loss of detail in this part of the video field. A bright window, therefore, may be shown as a featureless white rectangle on video, though the human eye may see trees and buildings outside the window. If too little light hits a pixel, there may be no electrical charge, or the charge may be too weak to be picked up as part of the video signal, again causing a loss of detail. A person standing in deep shadow may be visible to the human eye, but the shadow will be rendered in the video signal as featureless black and the person will not be seen.

The range from the darkest image that can be recorded to the brightest that can be handled is called the contrast range. The human eye has a very large contrast range. A person can see detail in deep shadow and also in sunshine that may be hundreds of times brighter. The brightest light that a video camera can handle is only 40 times brighter than the darkest. (The contrast range of a video camera is thus said to be approximately 40:1.) This means that to make a scene look natural and pleasing on video, light must be carefully controlled so that all brightness values fall within this very limited range.

If there is little light striking the chip, the video signal will be very weak and the image will be dark. This image can be made brighter by amplifying the strength, or *gain*, of the voltage. Making an image brighter by boosting the gain can result in an inferior image, because there are stray charges floating through any electrical system. Normally these stray charges are so small that they do not affect the video signal or the resulting image. If the signal is amplified, however, these slight charges can become strong enough to show up as "light" on the video image. These areas of random brightness are referred to as video noise. The more the signal is amplified, the noisier the image becomes. For this reason, it is better to adjust exposure using the lens than by adjusting video gain.

Though many video cameras display exposure in terms of f-stops, not all video lenses have physically adjustable irises. In some lower-end cameras the exposure control is actually a gain control, increasing or decreasing the sensitivity of the chip to light. In these cameras "opening up" actually boosts the gain, possibly resulting in a noisy image. High-end professional cameras with high-quality lenses have both an iris in the lens and a gain control on the camera, giving the filmmaker extensive control over exposure.

Many cameras have an automatic exposure control which measures the amount of light entering the lens and adjusts the iris or the gain to compensate. When shooting under bright conditions, the iris will be closed down or the gain lowered. When shooting under low-light conditions, the iris will be opened up or the gain will be boosted. As long as the camera is kept in autoexposure mode, the iris or gain control will constantly react to changing light. Overall, relying on the automatic iris can result in poorly exposed images.

Light Metering

Working in 16mm a filmmaker will always use a handheld light meter. The handheld meter can be a **reflected light meter**, an **incident light meter** or a combination of the two. Most super-8 cameras (and a few 16mm cameras) have a built-in light meter that controls the camera's lens iris when the camera is in its automatic mode. In effect these cameras combine two distinct instruments; a reflected light meter to measure light and a camera to take pictures. When the camera is in its automatic setting, the in-camera light meter reads the amount of light reflected by the subject, and then it automatically sets the lens iris to the indicated f-stop.

Every reflected light meter is built and calibrated upon a **medium gray** standard. These meters are designed so that they give a light reading (an f-stop number) that is the correct exposure to use when you want the subject read by the meter to be reproduced on the film in tones that are equivalent to medium gray (also known as **18% gray** or **neutral gray**). Reflected light meters usually have a wide angle of acceptance, and most shots include a variety of brightness, including light, dark and medium tones. A reflected light meter gives a reading based on an average of what it sees. In many cases the light, dark and medium tones within a shot do, in fact, average out to something close to the medium gray standard, and exposure will be correct.

In a scene which contains a range of brightness but is not dominated by very light or very dark objects, the light reflected by all the objects within the scene will average out to something close to

18% reflectance. In this case the light reading given by the reflected light meter will be correct. If you were to use the reflected light meter to take a reading from an object that reflects exactly 18% of the light striking it (for instance, an 18% **gray card**), the reading you would get would be the exact f-stop setting to use if you want that object to look medium gray on the film. However, if you were to take a reflected light reading from a black object (a black cat, for example) or from a scene dominated by dark tones, the f-stop reading you would get would result in overexposure. Instead of looking black on the film, the black cat would appear to be medium gray. Everything else would be brighter too. Similarly, a reflected light meter reading of a white scene (a snow-covered hill with a bright sky behind it) would give an f-stop reading that would result in underexposure. The white hillside and sky would look medium gray rather than white on the film. This problem can be overcome if you simply use the standard (18% gray) to which reflected light meters are calibrated.

To properly use an 18% gray card for reflected light readings, hold the card in the same light as the subject. The card must be angled to catch and reflect the light toward the camera position. The reflected light meter's field of view must be filled by the gray card. By taking a reflected light meter reading of an 18% gray card in this way and then manually adjusting the lens iris to the f-stop indicated, a filmmaker using a reflected light meter can avoid most of the pitfalls of this kind of metering system.

Incident light meters are preferred in most situations by the majority of filmmakers. These meters measure the amount of light *falling on* the subject rather than the light reflected by the subject. Using an incident meter a black cat, a white rabbit and an 18% gray card under the same light will all give the same reading. Like reflected light meters, incident light meters are built and calibrated upon a medium gray standard. An incident light meter measures the light falling on the subject, and it tells the filmmaker how to expose so that an 18% gray object under these lighting conditions would be

left: Taking a reflected light meter reading without a gray card.
right: The resulting exposure.

left: Taking a reflected light meter reading using a gray card.
right: The resulting exposure.

left: Taking an incident light meter reading.
right: The resulting exposure.

reproduced on the film looking like an 18% gray object. Objects that are lighter than medium gray will be reproduced lighter on the film and darker objects will be reproduced darker. In effect, an incident light meter is like a reflected light meter with a built-in gray card. A reflected meter used in conjunction with an 18% gray card will give the same readings an incident light meter gives.

While a reflected light meter's light-sensitive cell is pointed toward the subject (from the camera's position) in order to take a reading, an incident light meter is held at the subject's position and pointed toward the camera. An incident light meter's light-sensitive cell is usually covered by a translucent hemisphere (it looks like a small ping-pong ball, cut in half) that collects light from all side and front sources. This three-dimensional light collector actually simulates a three-dimensional gray card. The meter reading tells the filmmaker how to expose the film such that an 18% gray three-dimensional object would be accurately reproduced on the film.

An incident light meter will only indicate the amount of light falling on the subject. The filmmaker must determine the proper f-stop based on the shutter speed of the camera and the sensitivity of the film. (Some incident light meters make the calculations internally, while others require the user to manually calculate the appropriate f-stop.) The reflected light meter built into a super-8 camera makes these calculations automatically and indicates an f-stop number.

When shooting with a video camera, you can see the effect of changing exposure immediately and directly in the viewfinder. For this reason it is rare for someone to use a light meter when shooting video. A properly-calibrated viewfinder or external monitor is much more valuable than either a reflected or an incident light meter.

Focus

The basic function of a lens is to gather light rays and focus them onto the film or chip. By adjusting the glass elements in a lens, you can focus on objects at different distances from the camera; the numbers on the **focusing ring** of the lens indicate the distance the lens is focused on. If the focusing ring is set at ten feet, for instance, all objects on a plane ten feet away will appear to be **in focus**. The **plane of critical focus** is ten feet away. (Note: when measuring focus, one doesn't measure from the end of the lens, but from the **focal plane**. In a film camera this is the same as the **film plane**, which is marked on the side of the camera by a ⏀ symbol.) Objects in front of or behind the plane of critical focus will be **out of focus**; the farther they are from the plane of critical focus, the more out of focus they appear. Objects that are close to the plane of critical focus are so slightly out of focus that they *seem* to be in focus. Rather than just a flat plane being in focus, there is actually an area in front of and behind the plane of critical focus that appears to be in focus. This area, delineated by the near and far limits of acceptably sharp focus in a given situation, is known as the **depth of field**. Depth of field is not a constant. It can be a few inches, or it might be hundreds of feet. Depth of field depends upon three variables:

1. *Focal length*: Shorter (wide-angle) lenses provide greater depth of field than long (telephoto) lenses.

2. *F-stop*: Stopping down the iris increases depth of field; opening up decreases depth of field. Therefore, you will usually have less depth of field in low lighting, when the lens iris must be opened up.

3. *Focusing distance*: The farther the plane of critical focus, the greater the depth of field; the closer the camera is focused, the less the depth of field.

The final thing to keep in mind about depth of field is the "one-third two-thirds rule." That is, if there are two subjects at different distances from the camera that you want to have equally in focus, do not focus

Two shots with the same image size. Depth of field is much greater when using a wide-angle lens (top), than when using a telephoto lens (bottom).

halfway between them. The depth of field extends farther behind the plane of critical focus than it does in front of it, so as a general rule, focus on a point one-third of the way beyond the nearer of the two subjects.

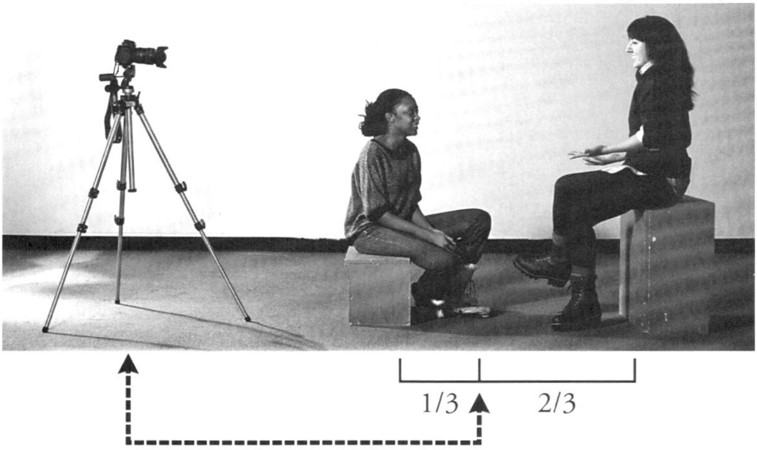

The one-third two-thirds rule. Focus is measured from the film plane in the camera to a point one-third of the distance beyond the nearer subject.

If the distance between camera and subject changes significantly during a shot, the filmmaker must **pull focus**, changing the focus while the camera is running in order to keep the subject in focus. Pulling focus may be required when either the camera or the subject is moving. If the movement is not very great and there is ample depth of field, it might not be necessary to pull focus.

The correct way to focus a zoom lens is to focus with the lens set at its longest focal length. Even if you are going to shoot a wide-angle shot of a person, zoom in on the person by turning the zoom ring on the lens to its extreme telephoto position. Adjust the focusing ring until this magnified image is sharp in the viewfinder. Then zoom out and compose the wide-angle shot. Every shot should be focused by following this procedure. Zoom lenses should always be focused at their longest focal length, because you can see greater detail when the image is magnified. Further, when the lens is in its telephoto position, depth of field is minimized and focus is most critical. The focusing distance does not change when the focal length is changed. Focus is dependent upon the distance between the camera and the subject.

Most video lenses also have an electronic feature called **autofocus**. When autofocus is engaged a sensor in the lens estimates distances to the object in the center of the frame and focuses to that distance. If the object or camera moves so that the distance changes, the autofocus re-focuses. In many situations this leads to a constant, random changing of focus distance, with certain objects becoming sharp or soft over and over. In general it is best to leave autofocus, like autoexposure, to people shooting home videos. A serious videomaker should control focus intentionally to direct audience attention to significant objects or areas of the frame.

Depth of Field Tables

Depth of field tables are used when shooting film in order to find the near and far limits of acceptably sharp focus. (When shooting video it is usually easier to see focus in the viewfinder and depth of field tables are not used). To obtain this information, use the tables for the format that you are using (16mm or super-8). Refer to the table for the focal length nearest the one you are shooting with. In that table find the column for the f-stop that you are using, and cross reference it with the appropriate corresponding row in the distance column (focusing distance). The numbers in the box where the column and the row intersect indicate the near and far limits of the depth of field for that specific combination of focal length, f-stop and focusing distance.

For example, in 16mm, shooting with a 25mm lens at f/2.8, focusing at 10 feet, the near limit is 8 feet 3 inches from the film plane; any object closer than that will appear out of focus. The far limit is 12 feet 7 inches from the film plane; any object farther away will appear out of focus. All objects between 8'3" and 12'7" will appear to be in focus. Keep in mind that depth of field falls off gradually. An object that is just outside the depth of field will be only slightly out of focus, while an object that is many feet beyond the depth of field will appear to be much more distinctly out of focus.

16 mm / Focal Length: 8mm

Distance	f/1.4 near far	f/2 near far	f/2.8 near far	f/4 near far	f/5.6 near far	f/8 near far	f/11 near far	f/16 near far
25’	7’ ∞	5’ ∞	4’ ∞	3’ ∞	2’ ∞	2’ ∞	1’ ∞	1’ ∞
15’	6’ ∞	5’ ∞	4’ ∞	3’ ∞	2’ ∞	2’ ∞	1’ ∞	1’ ∞
10’	5’ ∞	4’ ∞	3’ ∞	3’ ∞	2’ ∞	2’ ∞	1’ ∞	1’ ∞
8’	4’5” 43’	3’8” ∞	3’1” ∞	2’5” ∞	1’11” ∞	1’5” ∞	1’ ∞	0’9” ∞
5’	3’4” 10’1”	2’11” 18’	2’6” ∞	2’ ∞	1’7” ∞	1’3” ∞	1’ ∞	0’8” ∞
3’	2’4” 4’4”	2’1” 5’4”	1’10” 7’8”	1’7” 23’	1’4” ∞	1’ ∞	0’11” ∞	0’8” ∞
1’	0’11” 1’1”	0’11” 1’2”	0’10” 1’3”	0’9” 1’5”	0’9” 1’8”	0’8” 2’5”	0’7” 5’	0’6” ∞

16 mm / Focal Length: 10mm

Distance	f/1.4 near far	f/2 near far	f/2.8 near far	f/4 near far	f/5.6 near far	f/8 near far	f/11 near far	f/16 near far
50’	14’ ∞	10’ ∞	8’7” ∞	6’11” ∞	5’1” ∞	4’9” ∞	3’11” ∞	2’8” ∞
25’	10’1” ∞	5’2” ∞	3’11” ∞	2’11” ∞	2’2” ∞	1’7” ∞	1’2” ∞	0’10” ∞
15’	7’5” 84’	4’5” ∞	3’7” ∞	2’8” ∞	2’ ∞	1’6” ∞	1’2” ∞	0’10” ∞
10’	6’4” 15’6”	3’11” ∞	3’2” ∞	2’6” ∞	1’11” ∞	1’5” ∞	1’1” ∞	0’9” ∞
5’	4’1” 6’8”	2’11” 8’2”	2’4” ∞	2’1” ∞	1’9” ∞	1’3” ∞	0’11” ∞	0’9” ∞
3’	2’5” 3’1”	2’1” 5’6”	1’10” 8’4”	1’7” 33’2”	1’4” ∞	1’1” ∞	0’10” ∞	0’8” ∞
2’	1’9” 2’5”	1’6” 2’10”	1’5” 3’6”	1’3” 5’0”	1’1” 12’7”	0’11” ∞	0’9” ∞	0’7” ∞

16 mm / Focal Length: 12mm

Distance	f/1.4 near far	f/2 near far	f/2.8 near far	f/4 near far	f/5.6 near far	f/8 near far	f/11 near far	f/16 near far
25'	12’ ∞	10’ ∞	8’ ∞	6’ ∞	5’ ∞	3’ ∞	3’ ∞	2’ ∞
15'	9’ 46’	7’8” 465’	6’4” ∞	5’1” ∞	4’ ∞	3’ ∞	2’ ∞	2’ ∞
10'	6’11” 18’	6’1” 28’	5’3” 99’	4’5” ∞	3’7” ∞	2’10” ∞	2’2” ∞	1’8” ∞
5'	4’ 6’5”	3’9” 7’4”	3’5” 9’1”	3’ 13’11”	2’8” 573’	2’2” ∞	1’10” ∞	1’5” ∞
3'	2’8” 3’6”	2’6” 3’9”	2’5” 4’1”	2’2” 4’11”	1’11” 6’7”	1’8” 13’	1’5” ∞	1’2” ∞
2'	1’10” 2’3”	1’9” 2’4”	1’8” 2’5”	1’7” 2’9”	1’6” 3’2”	1’4” 4’2”	1’2” 6’11”	1’ ∞
1'	1’ 1’1”	0’11” 1’1”	0’11” 1’1”	0’11” 1’2”	0’10” 1’3”	0’10” 1’4”	0’9” 1’7”	0’8” 2’1”

16 mm / Focal Length: 16mm

Distance	f/1.4 near far	f/2 near far	f/2.8 near far	f/4 near far	f/5.6 near far	f/8 near far	f/11 near far	f/16 near far
25'	15’4” 69’	13’ 270’	11’ ∞	9’ ∞	7’ ∞	5’ ∞	4’ ∞	3’ ∞
15'	10’10” 24’3”	9’9” 33’	8’6” 63’	7’2” ∞	5’11” ∞	5’ ∞	4’ ∞	3’ ∞
10'	8’ 13’5”	7’4” 15’8”	6’8” 20’	5’10” 36’	5’ ∞	4’1” ∞	3’4” ∞	2’7” ∞
8'	6’8” 10’	6’2” 11’3”	5’8” 13’6”	5’1” 19’	4’5” 43’	3’8” ∞	3’1” ∞	2’5” ∞
6'	5’3” 7’1”	4’11” 7’8”	4’7” 8’8”	4’2” 10’7”	3’9” 15’4”	3’3” 46’	2’9” ∞	2’2” ∞
4'	3’8” 4’6”	3’6” 4’8”	3’4” 5”	3’1” 5’8”	2’10” 6’9”	2’6” 9’7”	2’3” 20’	1’10” ∞
2'	1’11” 2’1”	1’10” 2’2”	1’10” 2’3”	1’9” 2’4”	1’8” 2’6”	1’7” 2’10”	1’5” 3’4”	1’3” 4’9”

16 mm / Focal Length: 25mm

Distance	f/1.4 near far	f/2 near far	f/2.8 near far	f/4 near far	f/5.6 near far	f/8 near far	f/11 near far	f/16 near far
50'	33' 104'	29' 195'	25' ∞	20' ∞	16' ∞	13' ∞	10' ∞	7' ∞
25'	19'10" 33'9"	18'3" 40'	16'5" 52'	14' 98'	12' ∞	10' ∞	8' ∞	6' ∞
15'	13' 17'9"	12'3" 19'4"	11'5" 21'10"	10'5" 27'	9'3" 40'	7'11" 139'	6'9" ∞	5'5" ∞
10'	9'1" 11'2"	8'9" 11'9"	8'3" 12'7"	7'9" 14'3"	7'1" 17'2"	6'3" 25'	5'6" 55'	4'7" ∞
8'	7'5" 8'9"	7'2" 9'1"	6'10" 9'7"	6'6" 10'6"	6' 12'	5'5" 13'3"	4'10" 23'	4'1" 164'
5'	4'9" 5'3"	4'8" 5'4"	4'7" 5'7"	4'4" 5'10"	4'2" 6'4"	3'10" 7'1"	3'7" 8'5"	3'2" 12'4"
4'	3'10" 4'2"	3'10" 4'3"	3'9" 4'4"	3'7" 4'6"	3'5" 4'9"	3'3" 5'3"	3' 5'11"	2'9" 7'8"

16 mm / Focal Length: 50mm

Distance	f/1.4 near far	f/2 near far	f/2.8 near far	f/4 near far	f/5.6 near far	f/8 near far	f/11 near far	f/16 near far
25'	23'6" 26'9"	22'11" 22'7"	22'2" 28'9"	21'1" 30'8"	19'10" 33'9"	18'3" 40'	16'7" 51'	14' 97'
15'	14'7" 15'5"	14'3" 15'11"	13'11" 16'3"	13'6" 16'11"	13' 17'9"	12'3" 19'4"	11'6" 21'8"	10'5" 27'
10'	9'10" 10'2"	9'8" 10'5"	9'6" 10'7"	9'4" 10'10"	9'1" 11'2"	8'9" 11'9"	8'4" 12'7"	7'9" 14'3"
8'	7'10" 8'2"	7'9" 8'3"	7'8" 8'4"	7'7" 8'6"	7'5" 8'9"	7'2" 9'1"	6'11" 9'7"	6'6" 10'6"
6'	5'11" 6'1"	5'11" 6'2"	5'10" 6'2"	5'9" 6'4"	5'8" 6'5"	5'6" 6'7"	5'4" 6'10"	5'1" 7'4"
4'	4' 4'1"	3'11" 4'1"	3'11" 4'1"	3'11" 4'2"	3'10" 4'2"	3'9" 4'3"	3'9" 4'4"	3'7" 4'7"
2'	2' 2'	2' 2'	2' 2'	2' 2'	2' 2'1"	1'11" 2'1"	1'11" 2'1"	1'11" 2'2"

16 mm / Focal Length: 75mm

Distance	f/1.4 near far	f/2 near far	f/2.8 near far	f/4 near far	f/5.6 near far	f/8 near far	f/11 near far	f/16 near far
50’	45’7” 56’3”	44’ 57’11”	42’ 61’	39’3” 68’10”	36’2” 81’	32’4” 110’	28’7” 200’	23’11” ∞
25’	24’3” 25’9”	23’5” 26’10”	22’10” 27’8”	22’ 28’11”	21’ 30’11”	19’8” 34’4”	18’2” 39’11”	16’3” 54’7”
15’	14’7” 16’3”	14’5” 15’8”	14’2” 15’11”	13’10” 16’4”	13’6” 16’11”	12’11” 17’11”	12’3” 19’4”	11’4” 22’2”
10’	9’11” 10’2”	9’9” 10’3”	9’8” 10’5”	9’6” 10’7”	9’4” 10’10”	9’ 11’2”	8’9” 11’9”	8’3” 12’9”
8’	7’11” 8’1”	7’10” 8’2”	7’9” 8’3”	7’8” 8’4”	7’7” 8’6”	7’4” 8’9”	7’2” 9’1”	6’10” 9’8”
7’	6’11” 7’1”	6’10” 7’2”	6’10” 7’2”	6’9” 7’3”	6’8” 7’5”	6’6” 7’7”	6’4” 7’10”	6’1” 8’3”
5’	4’11” 5’1”	4’11” 5’1”	4’11” 5’1”	4’10” 5’2”	4’10” 5’2”	4’9” 5’3”	4’8” 5’5”	4’6” 5’7”

16 mm / Focal Length: 100mm

Distance	f/1.4 near far	f/2 near far	f/2.8 near far	f/4 near far	f/5.6 near far	f/8 near far	f/11 near far	f/16 near far
100’	93’11” 106’11”	92’ 110’	88’ 115’	84’ 123’	79’ 135’	73’ 159’	66’ 204’	57’ 389’
50’	48’5” 51’8”	47’9” 52’5”	47’ 53’6”	45’9” 55’1”	44’3” 57’6”	42’ 61’	40’ 67’	36’ 80’
25’	24’8” 25’5”	24’5” 25’7”	24’3” 25’10”	23’11” 26’3”	23’6” 26’9”	22’11” 27’7”	22’2” 28’8”	21’1” 30’8”
15’	14’11” 15’1”	14’10” 15’2”	14’9” 15’3”	14’7” 15’5”	14’6” 15’7”	14’3” 15’10”	13’11” 16’3”	13’6” 16’11”
10’	9’11” 10’1”	9’11” 10’1”	9’11” 10’1”	9’10” 10’2”	9’9” 10’3”	9’7” 10’4”	9’6” 10’6”	9’4” 10’9”
8’	8’ 8’	7’11” 8’1”	7’11” 8’1”	7’11” 8’1”	7’10” 8’2”	7’9” 8’3”	7’9” 8’4”	7’7” 8’6”
5’	6’ 6’	6’ 6’	6’ 6’	5’11” 6’1”	5’11” 6’1”	5’11” 6’1”	5’10” 6’2”	5’9” 6’3”

Super 8 / Focal length: 8mm

Distance	f/1.4 near far	f/2 near far	f/2.8 near far	f/4 near far	f/5.6 near far	f/8 near far	f/11 near far	f/16 near far
∞	7'10" ∞	5'7" ∞	4'1" ∞	3' ∞	2'3" ∞	1'8" ∞	1'3" ∞	1' ∞
35'	6'7" ∞	4'11" ∞	3'9" ∞	2'10" ∞	2'2" ∞	1'7" ∞	1'3" ∞	1' ∞
20'	5'10" ∞	4'6" ∞	3'6" ∞	2'8" ∞	2'1" ∞	1'7" ∞	1'3" ∞	1' ∞
10'	4'8" ∞	3'10" ∞	3'1" ∞	2'5" ∞	1'11" ∞	1'6" ∞	1'3" ∞	1' ∞
7'	3'11" 42'8"	3'4" ∞	2'10" ∞	2'3" ∞	1'10" ∞	1'8" ∞	1'2" ∞	0'11" ∞
5'	3'3" 11'4"	2'11" 26'7"	2'6" ∞	2'1" ∞	1'9" ∞	1'5" ∞	1'2" ∞	0'11" ∞
4'	2'10" 8'11"	2'7" 10'4"	2'3" 31'9"	1'11" ∞	1'8" ∞	1'4" ∞	1'2" ∞	0'11" ∞

Super 8 / Focal length: 12mm

Distance	f/1.4 near far	f/2 near far	f/2.8 near far	f/4 near far	f/5.6 near far	f/8 near far	f/11 near far	f/16 near far
∞	17'1" ∞	12' ∞	8'6" ∞	6'2" ∞	4'5" ∞	3'2" ∞	2'4" ∞	1'8" ∞
35'	11'8" ∞	9'2" ∞	7'1" ∞	5'4" ∞	4' ∞	3' ∞	2'3" ∞	1'8" ∞
20'	9'5" ∞	7'9" ∞	6'3" ∞	4'10" ∞	3'9" ∞	2'10" ∞	2'2" ∞	1'7" ∞
10'	6'6" 22'1"	5'8" 46'7"	4'10" ∞	4' ∞	3'3" ∞	2'7" ∞	2'1" ∞	1'7" ∞
7'	5'2" 11'1"	4'8" 14'10"	4'1" 27'3"	3'6" ∞	2'11" ∞	2'4" ∞	1'11" ∞	1'6" ∞
5'	4' 6'6"	3'9" 7'9"	3'4" 10'	3' 18'	2'7" ∞	2'2" ∞	1'9" ∞	1'5" ∞
4'	3'4" 4'11"	3'2" 5'6"	2'11" 6'6"	2'7" 6'11"	2'4" 17'11"	2' ∞	1'8" ∞	1'4" ∞

Super 8 / Focal length: 40mm

Distance	f/1.4 near far	f/2 near far	f/2.8 near far	f/4 near far	f/5.6 near far	f/8 near far	f/11 near far	f/16 near far
∞	240' ∞	210' ∞	150' ∞	105' ∞	75' ∞	52' ∞	38' ∞	26' ∞
50'	42'1" 62'9"	40'4" 65'9"	37'5" 75'3"	33'9" 96'	29'10" 152'	25'5" ∞	21'5" ∞	17' ∞
25'	22'9" 29'10"	21'7" 32'1"	20'11" 34'2"	19'8" 35'11"	18'1" 37'2"	17'5" 40'3"	15'10" 44'2"	14'9" 45'10"
10'	9'8" 10'5"	9'6" 10'6"	9'4" 10'9"	9'1" 11'1"	8'9" 11'7"	8'4" 12'6"	7'10" 13'9"	7'2" 16'6"
7'	6'10" 7'3"	6'9" 7'3"	6'8" 7'4"	6'6" 7'6"	6'4" 7'9"	6'2" 8'2"	5'10" 8'8"	5'5" 9'9"
5'	4'11" 5'1"	4'11" 5'2"	4'10" 5'2"	4'9" 5'3"	4'8" 5'5"	4'6" 5'7"	4'5" 5'10"	4'2" 6'3"
4	3'11" 4'1"	3'11" 4'1"	3'11" 4'1"	3'10" 4'2"	3'9" 4'3"	3'8" 4'4"	3'7" 4'6"	3'5" 4'10"

Super 8 / Focal length: 60mm

Distance	f/1.4 near far	f/2 near far	f/2.8 near far	f/4 near far	f/5.6 near far	f/8 near far	f/11 near far	f/16 near far
∞	421' ∞	294' ∞	210' ∞	147' ∞	105' ∞	73' ∞	52'10" ∞	36'1" ∞
35'	32'4" 38'2"	31'3" 39'9"	30' 42'	28'3" 48'10"	26'2" 52'4"	23'7" 66'2"	21' 98'7"	17'8" 211'
20'	19'1" 21'	18'9" 21'8"	18'3" 22'1"	17'7" 23'2"	16'9" 24'8"	15'8" 27'5"	14'5" 31'9"	12'10" 43'
10'	9'9" 10'3"	9'8" 10'4"	9'6" 10'6"	9'4" 10'9"	9'1" 11'1"	8'9" 11'7"	8'4" 12'4"	7'9" 13'9"
7'	6'11" 7'2"	6'10" 7'2"	6'9" 7'3"	6'8" 7'4"	6'6" 7'6"	6'4" 7'9"	6'2" 8'1"	5'9" 8'9"
5'	4'11" 5'1"	4'11" 5'1"	4'10" 5'2"	4'10" 5'2"	4'9" 5'3"	4'8" 5'5"	4'6" 5'7"	4'4" 5'11"
4	3'11" 4'1"	3'11" 4'1"	3'11" 4'1"	3'10" 4'2"	3'10" 4'2"	3'9" 4'3"	3'8" 4'5"	3'6" 4'7"

Chapter 5

Composition

The **frame** is the basic unit of visual material from which films are constructed. A continuous series of frames constitutes a **shot**. Each time the camera is turned on, a new shot is exposed or recorded. When the camera is turned off, or when the shot is cut in the editing process, the shot is over. Shots are edited together to build **scenes**. Any group of shots that is meant to be interpreted as being continuous in time and space constitutes a scene. A jump in space (e.g. from a character's bedroom to the street outside) or time (from the bedroom today to the same bedroom six months later) is usually interpreted as a change of scene. When shooting a film each shot is also referred to as a **camera take** or simply a **take**. A take can be described as the series of frames from camera start to camera stop.

Shots and Image Size

Shots are most often defined by the size of the subject within the frame. There are three basic types of shots. They are usually abbreviated in scripts and storyboards as follows:

LS: ***Long Shot***
MS: ***Medium Shot***
CU: ***Close-up***

When shooting footage of a person a long shot would show the entire person and a lot of the background. A medium shot might include the individual from head to waist. A close-up shot usually includes the person's head and shoulders. These are general guidelines. The different types of shots are *relative* to each other, and there are no strict rules.

Extreme Long Shot (ELS)

Long Shot (LS)

Medium Shot (MS)

Close-Up (CU)

Extreme Close-Up (ECU)

Of course, films are not constructed from only these three types of shots. A film or a scene made up of too many similar shots can be visually uninteresting. Most films contain a variety of shots and image sizes, ranging from extreme long shot to extreme close-up. There are many shot variations within the three basic types. The most commonly used shots are described as follows:

ECU: **Extreme Close-up.** ***If shooting a person's face an ECU might only reveal the person's eyes.***

MCU: **Medium Close-up.** ***This falls somewhere between medium shot and close-up.***

MLS: **Medium Long Shot.** ***This falls somewhere between medium shot and long shot.***

ELS: **Extreme Long Shot.** ***This would show the entire person within the environment. The person would be a very small part of the frame.***

Camera Angles

In addition to image size, camera angle must also be considered when setting up a shot. Shooting with the camera placed at an appropriate vertical angle to the subject is important in giving emphasis to the content of a shot. For instance, if the camera is placed at an angle above the subject (a **high angle shot**) the subject appears to be physically diminished. The action or object often takes on a sense of insignificance or vulnerability. The effect when photographing from a low angle is just the opposite. In a **low angle shot** the subject seems to have added importance or power and appears dominant in the frame.

Just as the camera's vertical angle affects the meaning of a shot, its horizontal placement is equally important. If the camera is placed squarely in front of the subject, shooting straight on, depth is minimized. The subject will appear to be relatively flat, less three-

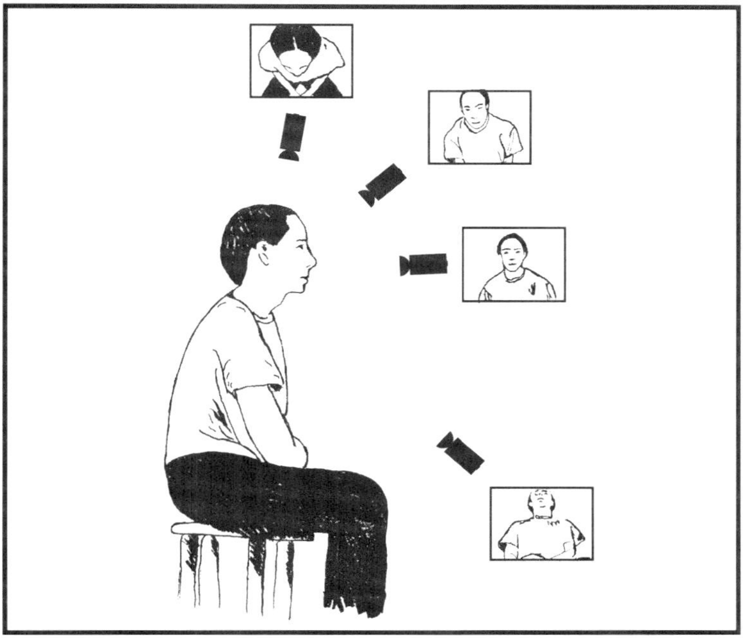

Vertical camera angles.

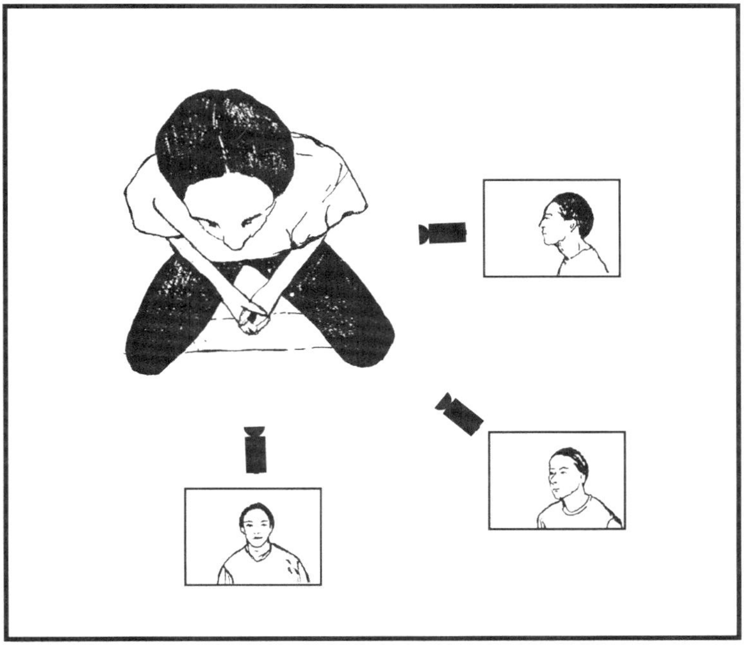

Horizontal camera angles.

dimensional. Moving the camera slightly to either side will allow a view of the front and one side of the subject simultaneously, adding apparent depth to the subject. If the camera is moved further to the side, so that only the side of the subject is visible and the front can no longer be seen, then the apparent depth of the shot is again diminished.

A filmmaker might also choose to tilt the camera slightly, creating a **Dutch angle shot**, which can create the feeling that the subject is unbalanced. Often evil characters or characters in dangerous circumstances are presented in Dutch angle shots, or such shots can be used to convey the instability of a situation. In his film *Do the Right Thing* (1989) filmmaker Spike Lee makes extensive use of Dutch angles as he portrays a neighborhood on the verge of violent collapse. Other films notable for their extensive use of Dutch angles include Carol Reed's *The Third Man* (1949) and Hal Hartley's *Fay Grim* (2006).

Dutch angle.

Compositional Guidelines

Cinematic composition, the arrangement of objects and light within the frame, is similar to composition in photographs or paintings. However, pictorial composition for film must also take movement into consideration. Objects within the frame are often in motion, the camera itself is often moving, or the focal length of the lens is being manipulated to alter the framing during a shot, creating dynamic, changing compositions. In addition, one shot is joined to another shot, creating a continuous sequence of compositions in flux.

Effective composition evolves out of an intuitive sense of balance and harmony. This intuition is grounded in everyday experience in relating to the physical world. The filmmaker arranges objects within the rectangular space of the frame. When viewing such a specific space, our attention is naturally drawn to the most active points of that space. In the case of a rectangular space our view is drawn toward the corners of the frame where the vertical and horizontal lines meet. These are the most active or visually interesting points in the space. Objects that are centered in the frame tend to seem static, because this kind of framing does not draw attention to the active points within the frame. A centered composition can create a sense of stability, but it is also viewed less actively, since the eyes of the viewer do not tend to move through the frame. Most of the time filmmakers are concerned with keeping the audience visually engaged by encouraging their eyes to scan the frame. A compositional guideline that exploits the tendency to scan to the corners of the frame is the **Rule of Thirds**.

The idea of the Rule of Thirds is to divide the frame horizontally and vertically into thirds. In effect another frame is created within the frame, reinforcing the natural tension of the corners. By placing objects of key interest (a person's face, for example) at one of the four points where the horizontal and vertical lines intersect, a filmmaker can draw the viewer's line of sight to the most significant elements within the shot.

Rule of Thirds.

Another idea to consider when composing shots is the notion of compositional dominance. Often certain elements within a composition seem to take visual precedence. The viewer naturally tends to seek out the most dominant or primary element in a composition, then moves on to scan secondary elements. In a narrative film some elements within a frame take on dominance simply because of the dramatic or narrative context of the shot. The human face almost always functions as a dominant element. Faces often express emotion, providing crucial information within a shot.

Color can serve as a dominant element. In his film *Interiors* (1978), Woody Allen designed and photographed the entire film in muted earthy tones of brown and green. This was done to reflect the personalities of the central family who are a dreary bunch of repressed, soul-searching intellectuals. Suddenly, a new character is introduced into this group, the father's flamboyant, life-loving girlfriend. She is a *dramatic* dominant because of her clashing personality. Allen costumed her in bright primary red, *visually* reinforcing her as a dominant element in contrast to the otherwise conservative color scheme of the shots.

The contrast between light and dark areas can also create compositional dominance. A very effective way to create an area of dominance within a composition is to increase the light in that area or on the subject. In Alfred Hitchcock's 1941 film, *Suspicion*, a man's wife suspects that he is trying to poison her. In a famous scene Hitchcock shows the man ascending a staircase carrying a glass of milk on a tray. Although the glass is the smallest object in the long shot, it becomes a dominant element because the glass itself is brighter than any other object in the frame. Hitchcock placed a small light bulb inside the glass, causing the milk to glow menacingly as the man approaches his sick wife's room. On the other hand, areas of darkness or shadow patterns within a shot can also serve as dominant compositional elements. Bernardo Bertolucci's 1969 film, *The Conformist*, includes a stunning scene in which a woman in a black-and-white striped dress dances in a room dramatically striped with light and shadow created by the room's Venetian blinds. The interplay between the stripes of the dress and the striped shadow pattern create a complex composition in which the woman is dominant as she moves through the frame, and a dynamic, changing pattern of light and dark lines moves over her.

Movement is one of the most powerful ways to call attention to an object or person. Moving objects attract the human eye. If one thing is moving in an otherwise static composition, it will usually become the single most dominant element of the shot. In Danny Boyle's 2003 film, *28 Days Later*, the protagonist awakens in a hospital to discover a deserted post-pandemic London. As he exits the hospital, there is an extreme high-angle static long shot. Although the man is a tiny figure, he is the dominant element within the shot because he is the only thing moving, emphasizing his isolation and the surrounding desolation. The opposite of this is also true. A stationary person surrounded by the hectic movement of a crowd will stand out as well.

Objects in the foreground of a shot, particularly a low angle shot, appear larger and therefore dominate the compositional scheme. However, filmmakers often place objects in the foreground of a shot even if they have no meaning in the dramatic context of the shot. The filmmaker might simply want to break up the foreground to lend a sense of depth to the shot or to make the frame more graphically interesting. Sharpness of focus can also affect compositional dominance. An area of the frame that is in sharper focus than the rest of the frame will naturally attract the viewer's attention, and filmmakers commonly use selective focus (slightly out-of-focus foreground and background surrounding a character crisply in focus) in order to exploit this tendency.

A composition using selective focus.

Composition Outside the Frame

Shots are often composed solely within the boundaries of the frame, with objects and action arranged in a way that takes into account only the rectangular space of the frame. However, it is frequently useful and even necessary to compose shots that make active use of the imaginary space that extends beyond the borders of the frame. Filmmakers often compose shots in which a portion of an important object appears at the edge of the frame. Since the rest of the object continues outside the boundaries of the frame, the audience is given a sense of the space that they do not actually see. People or objects moving into and out of the frame can also give the impression that space continues beyond the edges of the frame. Sounds that come from off screen can greatly enhance a viewer's tendency to picture more than just the images within the frame. The audience is encouraged, sometimes quite effectively, to imagine a much larger and more complex space than that which is defined by the edges of the screen.

A composition using off-screen space.

Camera Movement

Of course, the filmmaker has the additional consideration of movement when creating a shot. This might be the movement of an actor or an object through the frame while the camera is stationary, or it could be the motion created when the camera moves about a stationary object. Often both camera and subject are in motion.

If you are shooting a home movie it might be all right to carry the camera in your hand, waving it around to capture the action. Most home movies are shot **handheld**, but handheld shots are frequently shaky. A film with many unmotivated handheld shots can look amateurish, like a home movie. When shooting a landscape, a building or anything that doesn't move, the shot should be as steady as possible. Even the slight wobble that is evident in a relatively steady handheld shot can detract significantly from the shot's effectiveness, if you are shooting static objects. To keep the camera steady it can be mounted on a **tripod**, a three-legged support. Unless there is a reason for a handheld effect, it is always a good idea to use a tripod to steady the camera.

Just as a tripod allows you to take the steadiest possible **static shot**, a good tripod also enables you to move the camera smoothly. In order to **pan** (short for panorama shot), pivot the camera along its horizontal axis so that the frame moves to the left or the right. You can pan along the horizon to show a landscape, or pan along a car from front bumper to back bumper. You can also pan to follow the subject's movement; if an actor walks to the right to open a door, you can pan right, keeping her in frame as she moves to the door. A **tilt** is a movement in which the camera pivots along its vertical axis. You can tilt up from the base of a skyscraper to the top, or you can tilt down from an actor's face to her feet.

When executing a pan or tilt set yourself so that your body is in a comfortable, balanced position at the *end* of the pan or tilt, and then twist back into the beginning camera position. This way your body can slowly, steadily unwind through the camera movement. If you start out straight and twist into the pan or tilt, it will be harder to make the movement smooth because you will be moving into an unbalanced position.

In some situations it might not be practical to use a tripod. If you were shooting footage of the running of the bulls in Pamplona, it would be impossible to move the tripod from one position to another fast enough to keep up with the action. In these situations a handheld camera is necessary. In other situations handheld camera work is also an aesthetic choice that can add dynamism to a shot or scene. A handheld camera can be very effective when it is motivated by the demands of the film. In *Black Swan* (2010) Darren Aronofsky uses shaky handheld shots following the main character as she walks, adding a visual element that emphasizes the character's brittle, unstable state of mind. In Lars Von Triers' film *Breaking the Waves* (1996) handheld camera work is used to create a sense of chaos and emotional immediacy. While the exaggerated handheld camera of *Breaking the Waves* might be too extreme for some, this kind of camera work is commonly used to give fiction films a documentary feeling. The science-fiction movies *Cloverfield* (2008) and *District 9* (2009) are two good examples. Many action films, such as *Star Trek* (2009), use a constantly moving camera even in dialogue scenes and add violent camera shake or quick, seemingly random camera movements to action scenes.

If you are not using a handheld camera to create this kind of visual excitement, there are ways to make handheld shots steadier. As with any type of camera movement, it is necessary to rehearse handheld shots. When walking with the camera, keep your knees slightly bent so that they act as shock absorbers. Use short, even strides rather than long, bouncing ones. Keep your shoulders level; don't bounce up and down. The camera will move more smoothly and steadily. Handheld shots taken with a telephoto lens will usually appear shaky because long lenses magnify the image and any unsteadiness of the frame will be emphasized. Consequently, wide-angle lenses usually work best to make handheld work look smoother.

A comparison of a zoom in (left column) and a dolly in (right column). The perspective changes are very different in each sequence.

If you put the camera on wheels (a wheeled platform, a wheelchair, a car) you have a **dolly** which can be used to move the camera in many ways. You can dolly in toward the subject; the dolly-in to a close-up of a character's reaction in order to enhance the drama of the moment has become a commonly-used cinematic device. You can also start with a close-up and dolly out to show more of the setting or to add dramatic emphasis by revealing a crucial detail. You can dolly left or right to follow someone or you can dolly past a group of people waiting in line, from the front to the back of the line. A dolly shot, because it moves the camera through space, can be very dynamic and effective. However, if the dolly movement is shaky or uneven, the shot can look distracting and unprofessional. In that case a steady static shot might have been a better choice.

A **tracking shot** is a specific type of dolly shot in which the camera moves along with the subject. The camera might track left or right to follow a moving person, or it might track forward or backward, trailing or preceding a subject in motion. While the subject moves, the camera tracks with it, keeping it properly framed.

Even though a dolly in might seem to resemble a zoom in, it is actually very different. As the camera dollies toward a subject it moves through space. Perspective is constantly changing since the camera is constantly changing its position in relation to the objects in the frame. When the camera zooms in on a subject, the image is simply magnified. Objects in the foreground and the background are magnified equally. Perspective does not change since the camera stays in one position.

A Steadicam, Glidecam or similar device uses counterweights to smooth out the shaky movement of a handheld shot. Shooting with one of these camera mounts allows the operator to combine the smoothness of a dolly shot with the freedom and flexibility of a handheld camera.

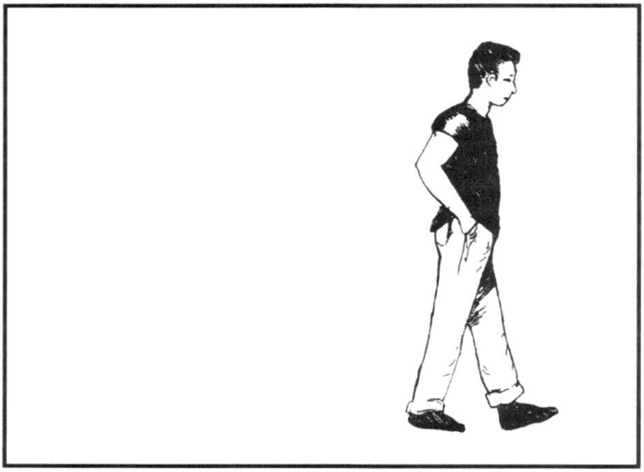

In this awkward composition, the character seems to be running into the edge of the frame.

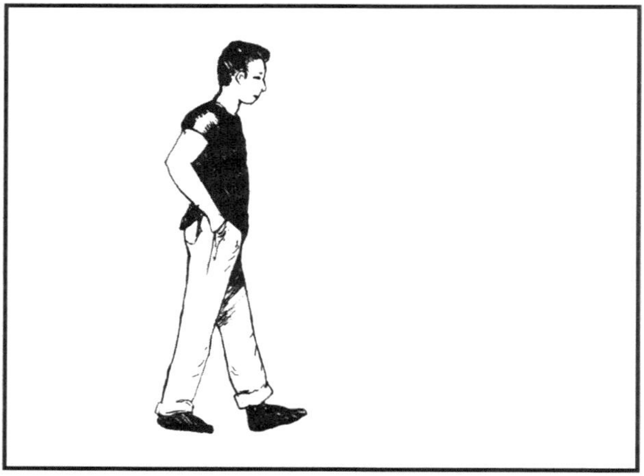

When the camera leads the action, the audience has a sense of the space the character is moving into. The composition seems more balanced.

Movement in the Shot

In addition to camera movement a filmmaker must also consider the movement of actors or objects through the frame. Choreographing this movement as well as any movement of the camera during a shot is referred to as **blocking**. In some cases blocking can be elaborate and considerations of framing and camera angle are important. Understanding the compositional space within the frame makes it easier to block movement to create the desired meaning or feeling for a shot. Because the corners of the frame tend to draw the viewer's attention, movement through the frame on a diagonal is more dynamic than movement on a vertical or horizontal line. In chase scenes and action sequences filmmakers often make use of diagonal movement through the frame from corner to corner to increase the feeling of movement. In contrast, consider a scene in which a group of people are lost in a desert. A filmmaker might depict the group moving through the shot on a horizontal line. This type of composition does not exploit the inherent visual tension within the frame and effectively emphasizes the expanse of the environment and the unbearable slowness of the group's progress. David O. Russell uses both types of shots effectively in his 1998 Gulf War film, *Three Kings.*

Another important compositional consideration when shooting a subject in motion is the concept of **leading the action**. When the camera follows a person walking down the street, it is important to allow space between the person in motion and the edge of the frame. Unless there is more space in front of the character than behind him, he will seem to be running into the boundary of the frame and the shot will feel confined. Leading the action helps give viewers a sense of the space outside the frame, the space the subject is moving into.

Head room should be considered when composing shots. Similar to the concept of leading the action, some space should be allowed above and below a person's head when composing a close-up. If the top of the head or the chin is too close to the frame line, the shot will seem confined because the edge of the frame is emphasized and the composition will seem unbalanced. When shooting an extreme close-up, "cutting off" a little bit of the top of the subject's head can result in a strong composition that conveys a sense of the space outside the frame. In the same way, when shooting close-ups of a subject looking screen right or screen left, space should exist between the person's face and the edge of the frame. The idea of allowing proper head room, not too little space but not too much either, applies to medium shots and long shots as well.

Too much head room *Proper head room* *Not enough head room*

The filmmaker might also choose to change focus during a shot in order to direct the viewer's attention. A shot of a person waiting for a telephone call could start with the phone in the foreground of the frame but out of focus, making it seem unimportant. When the phone rings, the filmmaker can **rack focus** so that the telephone comes into sharp focus and the background goes out of focus. For a rack focus to be most effective the depth of field must be very shallow, so there will be a distinct shift when the focus is changed. Shooting techniques like these work best when they are well rehearsed before shooting. Often the camera operator will need an assistant who has the responsibility of manipulating the lens' focusing ring during the shot.

Compositional conventions are concerned with a sense of bala. within the frame. The viewer intuitively attempts to harmonize the different elements within a composition into a cohesive picture. A filmmaker should use knowledge and understanding of compositional elements to create this balance, or if the scene so requires, to create a composition that is unbalanced. There are no hard and fast rules when it comes to creating effective compositions. Ultimately, the most successful compositions deal with the graphic needs of a shot (or scene) while simultaneously addressing considerations of meaning and content (narrative or otherwise). The best way to develop a good sense of composition is to study it on the screen.

Continuity

In most narrative films the filmmaker is attempting to create an on-screen reality by shooting actors, objects and places with specific spatial and temporal relationships. Later, the pieces of photographed reality (shots) can be edited together to produce an apparently seamless recreation of space and time that can seem almost as if the viewer is actually there experiencing it. This space and time continuum is a cinematic illusion created by careful shooting and editing. Maintaining these relationships is called preserving the **continuity**.

Space and Time on Screen

Film is at once realistic and deceiving when it is used to represent or recreate the world around us. Films are usually created with images of real buildings and real sunrises, as opposed to painted sets or theatrical lighting effects. When viewing these images of reality, with their apparent depth of space and continuity of time, you are actually seeing a pattern of light on a flat two-dimensional screen. If you tried to touch the image you would feel the flat screen, obliterating this "realistic" image. When a filmmaker tries to recreate three-dimensional space, it is actually an attempt to create an illusion of that space on a two-dimensional plane. The more thoroughly a filmmaker understands concepts such as composition, lighting, continuity and screen direction, the more effective and convincing this illusion will be.

Filmmakers are able to manipulate the way in which space is perceived. Through shot choice, composition, camera movement and editing a filmmaker can make a small room look large, the space between two people look closer than it actually is or create spatial relationships that do not really exist. If the script calls for a tropical beach in the middle of Iowa, the filmmaker can edit a shot of a person walking out the door of a house in Des Moines back to back with a shot of that person emerging from the doorway of a building on a Florida beach.

The perception of time is also easily altered in the filmmaking process. In fact, virtually every narrative and documentary film compresses actual time. Many films tell a story or portray events that take place over the course of a few days, weeks or even years, but the actual **running time** of a film can range from a few minutes to a few hours. On the screen several hours can be easily compressed into two or three short shots. For example, a sequence of two people having breakfast might begin with a shot showing the couple ordering their meals. This shot could be followed by a close-up of empty plates and coffee cups on the table. The final shot of the sequence might show the waiter bringing the check to the table. One or two hours have been compressed into three shots with a running time of several seconds.

Expansion of time is also used for effect in filmmaking. In Rob Reiner's film *Stand By Me* (1986) four boys make a dangerous decision to cross a long train trestle. As two of the boys reach the mid-point of the trestle, a locomotive approaches from behind. Using a variety of shots, including a long shot of the oncoming train with the running boys in the foreground, medium shots of the boys running, close-ups of the train, close-ups of the boys' running feet and shots of the other boys watching from the end of the bridge, the 90-second sequence depicts an action (the train crossing the 100-yard expanse) that would normally occur in less than ten seconds.

Closer examination of the sequence reveals that the first three times a cut is made to a shot containing the train, the train is actually almost in the same position on the tracks. The space between the train and the boys is essentially expanded by moving the train back to the beginning of the trestle the first few times it is shown. The shots that do not include the train allow for manipulation of the train's position within subsequent shots.

This raises an important point about the *apparent* continuity within a scene. It is often possible to "cheat," to manipulate the position of people or things within subsequent shots if the shots are separated by another shot or shots. This technique frequently works because viewers tend to perceive film space and time by subconsciously comparing a given shot only to those shots that immediately precede and follow it.

Through shot choice, composition and highly manipulative editing, the filmmaker draws out the suspense and makes the action take much longer than it would in reality. The train scene also contains a long shot in which the boys are in the foreground of the shot running directly toward the camera with the train visible behind them, seemingly in hot pursuit. The depth of this shot is compressed because it is photographed with an extremely long lens, and the train appears to be almost on top of the boys. In reality the train was much farther from the actors than it appears on the screen. This composition, with its flattened perspective, creates a spatial illusion that is very effective in heightening the suspense and apparent danger within the scene.

Screen Direction

Screen direction is a term used to refer to the direction of movement within the frame or to the direction a character or object is looking or facing within the frame. The camera offers a selectively photographed view of reality. When you shoot straight on at a person as she steps to her right, she will be moving toward the left-hand edge of the frame, or **screen left**, as you look through the camera or watch the projected film. If the individual takes a step to her left she will be moving **screen right**. Because the film frame converts reality to its own two-dimensional space, rules of screen direction have evolved which help maintain directional continuity and the audience's perception of three-dimensional space.

The 180-Degree Rule

A filmmaker must have an idea of the individual shots that will be used to create a scene when preparing to shoot. A scene depicting two people having breakfast might consist of three basic shots; a medium shot showing both people seated at a table and two close-ups, one of each person. In order to shoot and edit this scene effectively it is important to understand the **180-degree rule**.

Within any given sequence the filmmaker establishes an imaginary 180-degree line that is sometimes referred to as the "axis." This line is established based on the natural line or direction of action within the sequence. The camera's position must remain on one side of that line from shot to shot so that the filmmaker can edit the scene smoothly. All shots are taken from the same side of the 180-degree line. If the camera crosses the line, a mistake in screen direction will occur. In the breakfast scene referred to earlier the director might begin by establishing the line or axis. If two actors are seated directly across a table from one another, the line of sight between the two characters would serve as a natural 180-degree line:

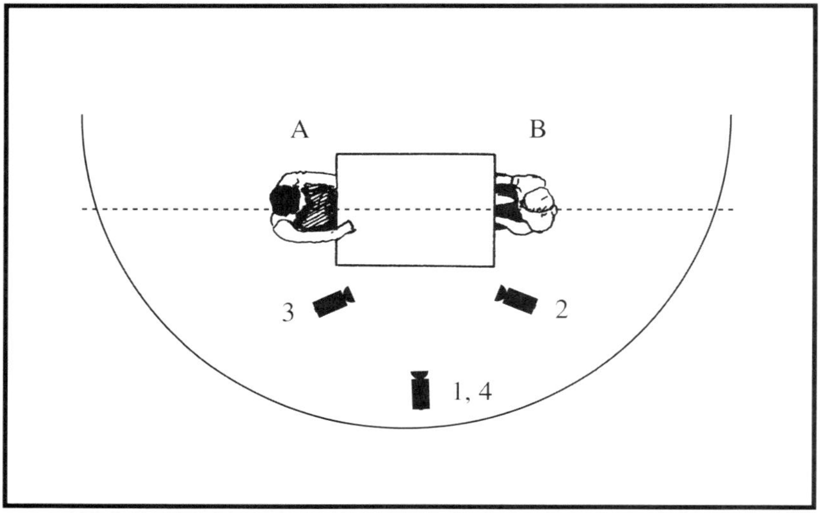

An overhead view showing the 180-degree line and three camera positions for a sequence of four shots. The numbers indicate the order of the shots in the edited sequence.

Suppose the filmmaker creates a four-shot sequence. The first shot is a medium shot of the two people at the table. This is followed by a close-up of character "A," then a close-up of character "B," and the sequence is completed with another medium shot. The series of shots would look like this:

1. MS, both characters

2. CU, character "A"

3. CU, character "B"

4. MS, both characters

The resulting sequence of shots when adhering to the 180-degree rule.

The overhead view on page 88 shows that the camera positions are all on the same side of the 180-degree line. However, if a shot is taken from a position on the wrong side of the line a mismatch in continuity will result (see the overhead view and resulting series of shots on page 90):

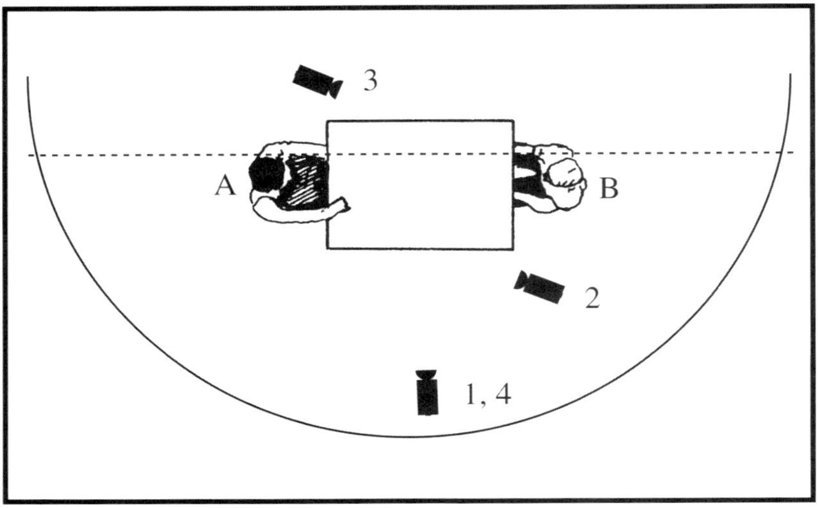

An overhead view showing the 180-degree line and three camera positions for a sequence of four shots. Camera position 3 is on the wrong side of the 180-degree line.

1. MS, both characters

2. CU, character "A"

3. CU, character "B"

4. MS, both characters

The resulting sequence of shots when breaking the 180-degree rule. In shot 3 character "B" is facing screen right, while in shots 1 and 4 he is facing screen left.

In the close-ups it appears as if the two characters are both looking in the same direction instead of looking at each other. This error in continuity is the result of positioning the camera on the wrong side of the line. To summarize the 180-degree rule, screen direction will be maintained if all shots are taken from one side or the other of the imaginary axis defined by the natural line of action within a sequence.

Changing Screen Direction

At times it is just as necessary to change screen direction as it is to maintain it. In most films the screen action does not move entirely in one direction. In general there are four ways to change screen direction within a scene or sequence.

1. *Changing Direction Within the Shot*
This method for altering screen direction is the most obvious. Simply show the subject changing direction within the shot. Once you have established a new screen direction, you will be concerned with preserving the continuity of the new direction.

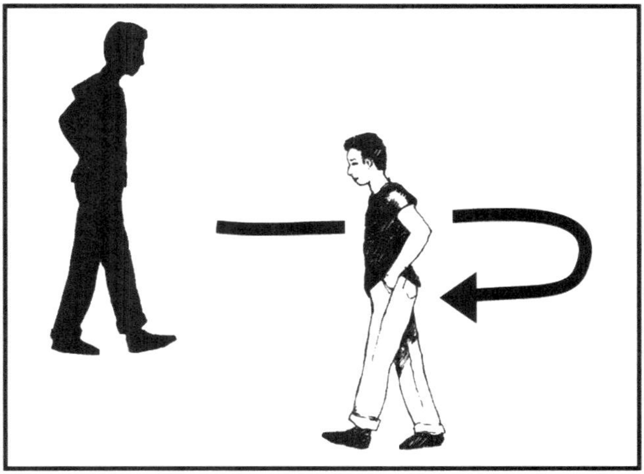

Changing direction within a shot.

Two shots separated by a cutaway shot.

2. *The Cutaway*

If there are two shots taken from opposite sides of the 180-degree line, and you want to maintain believable continuity and avoid confusing the audience, you will want to avoid using these shots back to back. Sometimes, because of the demands of the story, two mismatched shots will have to be used one after the other. A simple way to avoid this dilemma is to separate the two problematic shots by putting another shot (or several shots) between them. An audience watching a film tends to remember and be most affected by the physical relationships between any given shot and the shots that immediately precede and follow it.

A **cutaway** is a shot of something related to but outside of the immediate action of the scene. In the scene of two people eating breakfast a cutaway might be a shot of another person in the room. If you cut from the medium shot of one of the diners to this sort of cutaway, then you can cut to a shot taken from the other side of the 180-degree line without creating a mismatched cut.

Most of the time cutaway shots are used to add detail and meaning to a scene. However, cutaways can also be very useful in masking screen direction mistakes or mistakes in continuity. Filmmakers often shoot cutaway shots (even if they are not really crucial to the scene) to use in case they are necessary to cover problems in continuity or screen direction. In addition, cutaway shots also enable an editor to expand or contract the length of a scene.

3. *Neutral Angle*

Using the same strategy of separating two problematic shots by putting something between them, a filmmaker can cut to a shot with neutral screen direction, favoring neither screen left nor screen right. A **neutral angle** shot is taken with the camera positioned *on* the 180-degree line. In a sequence of a man walking down the street, the first shot establishes that the man is moving from screen left to screen right:

if the second shot is a neutral angle:

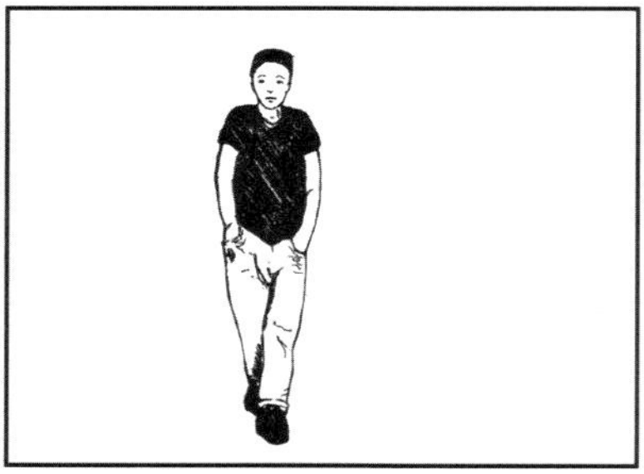

then you can use a shot of the man moving from screen right to screen left as the third shot:

In such a sequence of shots the change of screen direction from the first shot to the third shot is masked by the neutral angle shot between them. The audience understands that the man is continuing to make progress in the same direction, even though screen direction has changed.

4. *Camera Movement Across the Line*
If a shot from one side of the 180-degree line must be mixed with material shot from the other side of the line, another way to avoid screen direction problems is to show the change of orientation within a shot. That is, a filmmaker might use a transitional shot that actually shows the changing of screen direction relationships as the camera moves (either on a dolly or handheld) from a position on one side of the 180-degree line to a position on the other side of the line. The audience sees the change in spatial orientation as it occurs and will not be confused when the filmmaker cuts to the next shot, which must now maintain continuity with the new camera position on the other side of the line.

More About Continuity

Apart from making sure the camera stays on the correct side of the 180-degree line, it is also necessary to vary the camera position and/or the size of the subject in the frame. In the sequence of the man walking down the street, if the first shot is a long shot of the person walking along the street and the next shot is also a long shot from approximately the same position, the shots will not cut together smoothly and the action on screen will jump:

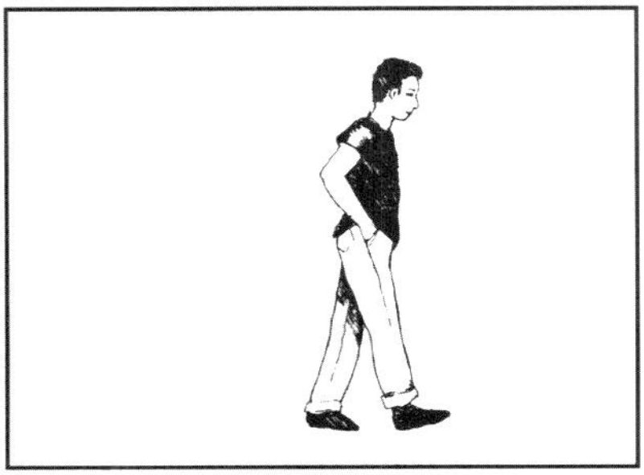

But if the position of the camera is significantly altered for the second shot, even if the image size is the same, the shots are more likely to go together smoothly:

If you keep the camera in the same position but significantly alter the image size, once again the shots should cut together well:

It is often best to change both the camera angle and the image size:

Overlapping Action and Master Shots

Finally, when shooting a series of shots intended to be edited together for continuity, the filmmaker should shoot **overlapping action**. In the breakfast scene discussed previously, the first shot is a medium shot of two people. If the second shot is a close-up of a person raising a cup to her mouth, she would lift the cup at the end of the medium shot as well as at the beginning of the close-up. This overlap of action from the end of one shot to the beginning of the next shot provides a range of choices during editing while alowing the editor to maintain the continuity of the action in the scene. If the action is not overlapped during shooting, then the choices available during editing are severely limited.

Frequently, action scenes are shot using a **master shot**. The master shot is a single take of the entire scene or sequence and is usually a long shot that shows the action from beginning to end. Its purpose is to provide total coverage for the sequence, and it is almost always intended to be used in combination with a number of other shots that show various details of the action. While an editor might only use several small pieces from a long master shot, it can be an invaluable source of backup material. If some other shot or shots are unusable for any reason, it is always possible to cut back to the master shot. It is seldom intended to be used in its entirety, and if some part of it is imperfect, it is not usually necessary to reshoot the entire master shot. Some scenes are edited using overlapping action; some are edited using master shot technique; many are edited using a combination of the two.

Chapter 7:

Editing Theory

The earliest films were one-shot films. The filmmaker set up the camera and recorded the action as it unfolded in a single long shot. As films became more sophisticated the action could not be contained in one shot, and so several of these uncut shots were joined together to tell the story, each shot being continuous like a scene in a play. Soon filmmakers learned they could break these scenes into pieces or shots that could be put together in an order other than that in which they were photographed. The finished film looked very different from the uncut camera takes. **Editing** is the process of selecting, cutting apart and joining together various shots.

Often a series of shots is necessary to convey information or to move quickly through time and space. In a scene in which someone is reading a letter the filmmaker might choose to make an edit, or **cut**, from a shot of the person's face to a close-up of the letter so that the audience can read it. If the scene is about a process or a progression of action such as building a house, the filmmaker can control the pacing of the action and can direct the audience's attention through editing. Editing enables a filmmaker to concentrate the viewer's attention on the most important aspects of the action.

If you were to observe a man arriving at home at the end of the day, the sequence of action might be quite long. The man drives his car up to the house, shuts off the engine, gets out of the car and locks it, walks to the house, unlocks the door and enters the house. An edited sequence depicting this event doesn't have to show every detail of the action. If there is a cut from a shot of the car stopping in front of the house to a different shot as the man enters the house, the audience can easily fill in the missing action. These small compressions of time occur frequently in edited sequences and can help the action move at a faster pace.

Although there are many ways to edit a film, every time two shots are spliced together or a piece is cut out of a shot, real time and space are altered to create the time and space of the film. In the sequence of the man entering his house, the editing condenses a specific period of time (the time it takes the man to get out of the car, walk to the house and unlock the door) into a substantially shorter period of time on film. The space is also redefined in that the man can be in the car at one moment and walking through the doorway of the house at the next instant. These ellipses in time and space create a flow of action that holds the audience's interest.

A scene's *pacing* depends on the lengths of the shots within the scene, but editing *rhythm* is also important. While pacing is primarily concerned with the pattern of shot lengths, the rhythm within a scene is created by a number of factors, including the speed and direction of movement within individual shots and the lengths of individual shots. Some of the more obvious examples of effective use of editing rhythm can be found in chase scenes. Often in such scenes the shots get shorter and the cuts come faster as the chase reaches its climax. At the same time, movement within the shots is usually at its most pronounced and frantic during the scene's climactic moments.

Invasion of the Body Snatchers, Don Siegel's 1956 low-budget science fiction classic, provides a typical example during a scene in which the film's two protagonists are being chased by a horde of inhuman alien look-alikes who have replaced the townspeople. This 27-shot scene begins slowly with longer shot lengths, picks up dramatically in the middle of the scene and slows down again toward the end.

The ten shots in the middle of the scene, as the chase reaches its climax, have average lengths that are only half as long as the shots that open and close the sequence. In a scene like this, as the pacing and rhythm of the editing picks up, the audience's heightened anticipation of what is to come next increases the scene's excitement. As the chase winds down the shots become longer and the pace slower, giving the audience time to catch its breath. Of course, rhythm is a factor in every scene. It is simply more pronounced and easier to grasp as a concept in a chase scene.

Continuity Editing

Often when editing a scene a filmmaker wants time and space to seem to be uninterrupted. In cutting from a long shot of a woman picking up a cup to a close-up as she is drinking from it, the filmmaker might want the gesture to appear smooth and continuous, like a single action, even though two shots (one long shot and one close-up) created the action. A scene in a film might consist of several shots, but the edited result can seem to be a continuous, unbroken sequence of action with no apparent jumps in space or time. **Continuity editing** tries to achieve this smooth, unobtrusive quality. Its goal is to move the film forward without calling attention to the editing process, preserving the illusion of reality that a film creates on the screen.

In good continuity editing the cuts are virtually invisible. This is often achieved largely with **match cuts**. Match cuts maintain continuity of action or movement from one shot to the next. They match screen position, timing and direction of movement to create an illusion of continuous movement within a sequence that actually consists of a number of shots. Match cuts lead the viewer's eye across the frame, following the movement of the action and making the edits appear seamless.

Unlike a match cut, a **jump cut** is a jarring cut that calls attention to itself. A jump cut can be the result of an edit between two shots in which there is too small a change in the image size or the camera angle (or both) resulting in a slight, but very noticeable, displacement of the image on the screen. Jump cuts make the viewer aware of the editing process. They tend to be awkward and can break the film's illusory spell. Of course, there may be times when that is exactly what you want to do. Jean-Luc Godard's influential film *Breathless* (1959) was one of the first to make extensive intentional use of jump cuts. The use of jump cuts as an editing strategy has become much more common in films and television today.

In order to make a successful match cut between two shots it is necessary to overlap the action during shooting (see Chapter 6, *Continuity*). Ideally, if time and budget permit, both shots should encompass the entire action and some time before it begins and after it ends. While this is not practical in every case, it does provide the maximum in creative options. You can choose to cut from one shot to the next before the action begins; you can make a match cut in the middle of the action; or you can cut after the action or movement has ended. If the entire action was photographed twice, you will have the ability to cut between the two shots at any point, and you will have greater freedom to consider important factors such as screen position and the direction of movement. There are a number of ways to make a successful match cut:

Change the image size significantly: If you cut from a long shot of a woman picking up a cup to a close-up in which just her face is seen as she drinks, it is difficult for the audience to notice small continuity differences in the shots, because the image size in the two shots is so different. If you cut from a medium shot to a slightly wider medium shot, there would be little change in image size. Inconsistencies in the woman's facial expression or body position or a jump or a repetition in her movement would be easily detected. Image size can be changed by either moving the camera relative to the subject or by changing the focal length of the lens.

Change the camera angle significantly: The general rule is that a change of camera angle of at least 30 degrees causes a significant enough change in the background and makes any jumps in action at the point of the cut less perceptible to the audience. For example, you might want to edit two close-ups of the woman back to back. If the first one is shot facing her straight on, shoot the second one from an angle off to one side.

Cut on action: Usually the best place to make the edit is while the woman is picking up the cup. The movement of her hand catches the viewer's attention and moves the viewer's eye smoothly across the frame. When cutting on action it is important to be aware of and to maintain both image placement and the direction of movement from one shot to the next. By effectively matching the position and direction of physical movement from one shot to the next, across the cut, your editing will become more fluid.

It is usually best to use a combination of these guidelines. Often it is most effective to change the image size and the camera angle while cutting on action. Sometimes, even if you are following these guidelines, no matter how you try to cut them, two shots will not work together smoothly. In the example of the woman drinking, the woman's head position might be significantly different from one shot to the next shot. Details of the set or her costume might have changed. In this situation you might use a cutaway shot to try to preserve the continuity of the scene. You might cut from the long shot to a shot of another person in the room and then to the woman's close-up. Since the shot of the other person doesn't involve any of the details of the main action that the other two shots have in common, it provides a possible way to avoid a bad cut that interrupts the flow of action and breaks the cinematic illusion.

When edited for continuity most scenes include, within the first few shots, an **establishing shot** in which everyone and everything is shown in relation to everyone and everything else. This is almost always a long shot and its purpose is to define the physical space. Once the space has been established the filmmaker is able to break it down into a variety of shots including close-ups and medium shots. If spatial relationships change significantly later in the scene (perhaps someone else enters the room) the filmmaker usually returns to another establishing shot so that the audience can see the new spatial relationships. Establishing shots are also frequently used as a transition to a new scene.

These editing techniques give the filmmaker the maximum range of choices when cutting a scene for continuity. If you are careful, plan your shoot in advance and cover the action in several shots, you will give yourself the opportunity to be creative in the editing room instead of being limited to only a few shots that can be edited effectively.

Alternatives to Continuity

Continuity editing is only one approach to editing, one that works best in certain types of films, particularly in conventional narrative films. In documentaries continuity editing is not usually necessary or even desirable. If the Boston Marathon is the subject of a film, the runners aren't going to repeat their actions after a change of focal length or camera angle. Various editing styles and techniques have been developed by filmmakers who sought to exploit film's ability to manipulate time and space in more pronounced ways.

Parallel editing is an editing technique that involves cutting back and forth between any two (or more) scenes or actions in order to suggest that these events are happening at the same time. Parallel editing is widely used and is very effective in establishing and building dramatic tension. Virtually every action movie makes use of parallel editing. The concept is simple. Two or more events, supposedly occurring simultaneously, are depicted by cutting back and forth between them a number of times. Every time it is shown, each event unfolds a little further. It seems as if both events are happening at the same time. In the well-known final sequence of Mike Nichols' *The Graduate* (1967) the main character, Ben Braddock, is racing to stop his girlfriend Elaine from marrying another man. The sequence was edited by cutting back and forth between shots of the wedding ceremony progressing and shots of Ben trying desperately to reach the church in time to stop the ceremony. The back-and-forth editing creates the sense that the two actions are occurring simultaneously.

In *The Godfather* (1972) Francis Ford Coppola makes good use of parallel editing in another kind of sequence. As Michael Corleone stands in a church witnessing the baptism of his godchild, Coppola cuts back and forth between shots in the church and various shots of Corleone's enemies being brutally slaughtered by his hit men. This memorable sequence conveys a sense of horror and irony as the shots of an angelic Michael Corleone are quickly intercut with shots of the bloodbath he has engineered.

In the example from *The Godfather*, parallel editing is used in conjunction with **montage** editing. The term "montage" is commonly used to describe virtually any sequence comprised of many brief shots. But montage is more than just a lot of quick flashy cutting. For some the term simply refers to the editing process ("montage" is the French word for editing), but the early Russian filmmaker and theorist Sergei Eisenstein defined montage as a "collision" of shots (and sounds and ideas) that creates something new. The juxtaposition of shots in a good montage creates meaning that the individual shots cannot convey alone.

Nicholas Roeg's 1973 film, *Don't Look Now*, involves a character who has visions of the future but doesn't recognize them as such. The film's final sequence includes an extended montage of about 100 seconds' duration and more than 60 shots. While the protagonist lies bleeding on the ground, many of the film's ambiguous but haunting images are tied together as they flash through his mind. Images of the present, his memories of past events, his previously misunderstood visions of the future and his visions of a future yet to come all converge on the viewer in a rapid-fire sequence that is the key to understanding the entire narrative. Most of the shots in this sequence already have a context within the film. Presented in this way and in this order, they achieve new meaning.

Montage is very different from the invisible editing of the continuity technique. Montage tends to emphasize the cuts, creating a visual collision of shots. The famous shower murder scene in Alfred Hitchcock's *Psycho* (1960) is a montage sequence of more than 70 shots edited into approximately 45 seconds of screen time. The terrible violence of the scene is not conveyed by the content of individual shots. There are few shots in the scene which contain both the victim and the knife and only one shot in which the knife appears to touch the victim's body. The stabbing is created through editing in which repeated shots of the knife flashing through the frame are quickly intercut with shots of the victim's reaction. The narrative content of the scene, the slashing of the victim, is visually amplified through the violent cutting of the film itself.

Any editing style implies that some actions or pieces of time are more important than others. The actions that are shown are obviously given greater importance than those that are not shown. In the **long take** style of filmmaking no single moment is intrinsically more important than any other. Rather than cutting shots into pieces and only using some of these pieces, the filmmaker uses long, uninterrupted camera takes, keeping the seemingly insignificant moments as well as the important ones. *Russian Ark* (2002) consists of a single tightly choreographed shot that lasts over 90 minutes. The resulting film is much slower than a tightly edited film like *Run Lola Run* (1999) or *The Dark Knight* (2008). Some of Andy Warhol's early films, like *Empire* (1964) and *Vinyl* (1965), take the long take style to the extreme. *Empire*, for example, consists of a single static shot of the Empire State Building for more than eight hours. In these films all of the film that was shot is included, even the fogged ends of each roll of film. It is the *absence* of editing, the apparent lack of manipulation, that makes the long take approach a unique editing style.

Chapter 8

Editing Mechanics

In one sense editing is a simple set of actions. For many years these were mechanical actions, as the strip of film was physically cut and the pieces were taped together in a new order. Today, most editing is done on computers that manipulate images as digital information, regardless of whether that information was transferred from film or videotape or originated as a digital file. The editing process, established through 100 years of practice in the film world, is essentially the same in the digital realm, even if the mechanics are vastly different. This chapter begins by discussing the basics of the process of physically editing film. Some filmmakers continue to work in that way for aesthetic reasons, but digital editing has become the dominant mode, and this chapter devotes a greater part of the discussion to the details of digital editing. The chapter also lays out some specific routes filmmakers follow when shooting film and editing digitally with the intention of distributing the finished product in either a digital format or as a film print.

Film Editing

When editing reversal film, a filmmaker usually projects the original uncut footage, called **rushes**, and selects the best takes. Rushes are sometimes referred to as **dailies**, and the terms are used almost interchangeably. If the film is shot on 16mm negative and the rushes are in the form of a positive film workprint made from that negative, the filmmaker begins by watching the material (preferably projected large) and makes notes. The next step is to select the best takes and put them together. In the editing room the rushes are screened again on an editing **viewer**, and the selected takes are marked for cutting. Using a **splicer** entire shots are cut out and hung in a bin in the approximate order that they will appear in the final film. The unused takes that remain are called **outtakes** and are stored on a separate reel in case they are needed later. Once the selected shots have been arranged in order, they can be taped together, or **spliced**, into an **assembly**, the first rough edit of a film.

Since it consists of entire takes that have been spliced together, the assembly will contain repeated action that needs to be cut out. After viewing the assembly and evaluating the film's basic structure it can be edited, putting pieces of various shots into their proper places and cutting out parts of shots that are not needed. The frames of film that are cut from the selected shots throughout the editing process are called **trims**. The trims are organized and saved in case they are needed later to adjust the length of a shot.

Once shots have been edited into their basic order, with repeated action removed, the film can be considered a **rough cut**. At this point the film should be watched again. It is important to view the film frequently during the editing process. When the shots have been edited to exactly the right length and the pacing and rhythm of the film have been established, the rough cut has become a **fine cut**.

If the camera original has been edited and is intended to be projected, then creative editing is complete and the film can be prepared for presentation. It is a good practice to put several feet of white **leader** (blank white film) at the **head** (the beginning) of the film and several feet of white leader at the **tail** (the end). This will help protect the edited footage. It is also a good idea to include some black leader at the head and tail of the film. Splicing a few seconds of black leader between the white head leader and the first image of the film, and putting another few seconds of black leader between the last image of the film and the white tail leader will cause the screen to go black before the first image or title appears and after the film's final image. Visually, this is a better opening for a film than cutting from the bright, white leader to the first shot. Including black leader at the end, after the last shot or title, is also more visually effective than going right into the white leader.

If a filmmaker has edited a workprint rather than the camera original, then before the film can be finished the camera original must be cut to match the edited workprint. **Conforming** is the process of carefully cutting the camera original to match the edited version of the film frame for frame. The film is conformed by using the **latent edge numbers** that appear outside the picture area along one edge of the strip of film. Latent edge numbers are a set of numbers that are photographically incorporated into 16mm and 35mm (but not super-8) film stock during manufacturing. Latent edge numbers are progressive, increasing by one digit every 20 frames on 16mm camera original, regardless of whether the original is negative or reversal. When the film is processed the latent edge numbers become visible. When a workprint is made the edge numbers are also printed onto the edge of the workprint so that the workprint is not only a frame-for-frame copy of the image, but an exact copy of the edge numbers as well. The filmmaker can then look at the edge numbers on the edited workprint and use those numbers to cut the exact frames needed from the camera original.

The conformed camera original is taken to a film laboratory where it is used to create an **answer print**. An answer print is the first finished print of an edited film and it contains no splices. If the camera original has been handled properly during conforming, the answer print will be free of dirt and scratches. When a film is printed the laboratory has the ability to make corrections to the color and exposure of individual shots. Such printing adjustments are known as **timing** (or **grading**) changes. Once the filmmaker has projected and approved the answer print with all its corrections, additional prints, called **release prints**, can be made from the camera original if necessary. All of the timing changes approved in the answer print will be incorporated into the release prints, the prints that are projected for the public.

Linear Video Editing

Video can be edited in one of two ways. A **linear editing system** uses multiple videotape decks to re-record the material to new tapes in a new order. A **non-linear editing system** uses a computer's random access capability to edit video as digital files that can be easily manipulated with no loss of quality. While linear video editing has become increasingly rare, its basic concepts have greatly influenced the layout and workflow of non-linear editing systems.

A simple linear system consists of a **source deck** that plays back the original material, a **record deck** which is used to record parts of the original material onto a new tape and an **edit controller** that allows the editor to control the two decks separately or in unison. In addition, each deck has its own monitor so that the editor can locate the proper point on each tape, preview shots to be selected and review the new order of shots on the new tape. A more complex linear **editing suite** would have multiple source decks and a **video switcher** to create dissolves, wipes and other complicated effects and transitions. A linear system without a switcher cannot be used to create these transitions and so is often referred to as a "cuts-only editing system."

When a shot or a piece of audio needs to be replaced or inserted into a nearly completed tape, the weakness of linear editing becomes apparent. Suppose that after editing a scene, the editor decides that the scene should begin with a new shot. This new shot cannot actually be inserted before the first shot on the tape, because the shots already on tape cannot be shifted to a new position. Since there is no way to shift the shots to a later portion of the tape, a new tape must be placed in the record deck and the scene edited again from the beginning, now with the new shot coming first.

One way to avoid these problems while still using linear editing systems is to make all of the initial decisions and changes on a working copy which will never be shown to an audience. The editing process involves making decisions, changing your mind after seeing the result, making new decisions and making new changes. Rather than go through this process in a high-quality editing suite that costs hundreds of dollars per hour to rent, an editor may edit on a lower-quality format in a lower-cost editing suite. This is known as **off-line editing**.

The end products of an off-line edit are a low-quality videotape that can be used as a reference and a much more important **edit-decision list** (**EDL**). An edit-decision list is a printout of every shot in the edited tape, the starting and ending timecode numbers of that shot on its source tape and the transition that joins them together. The EDL and the source tapes can be brought to an **on-line editing session** in an expensive editing suite using the same format (or a higher-quality format) as the source tapes. The on-line session involves simply using the EDL as a blueprint showing which parts of the various source tapes to use to build a new high-quality copy of the low-quality off-line version. While that version may have taken days or weeks to complete, the on-line edit can be made in a matter of hours. The final edited tape created on an on-line system is known as the **master tape**. Duplicates, or dubs, can be made from this master in various formats for distribution and exhibition.

Non-linear Editing

While some high-end on-line editing is still performed on linear systems, most video editing is now done on non-linear editing systems. A simple nonlinear editing system consists of a computer running an editing software application such as Apple's Final Cut, Adobe's Premiere or programs made by Avid Technologies. More complex systems can have extra hard drives for more digital storage, a video monitor (standard definition or high definition), high quality speakers for audio monitoring and one or more video decks or connections to get video into and out of the computer.

In non-linear editing, the first step is to get the video and audio information into the computer system, usually by connecting a camera or video deck to the computer. If the video is analog then it will need to be **digitized**. The editing software will sample the video and audio signals as the tape is played and turn them into digital information. Digital video, of course, already exists as binary numbers on the tape or storage device and simply has to be transferred to the computer. If an editor is capturing video or audio from a digital tape, the camera or deck plays the tape while the editor selects those portions of the footage that will actually be used for editing. In order to save storage space, only the selected material is captured to the computer's hard drive. If the video and audio was recorded as digital files on a memory card or hard drive the editor selects those files that will be used and copies them to the computer's hard drive.

When video and audio information is digitized or captured to a hard drive, **media files** are created. A media file is the actual set of 1s and 0s that make up the video and audio information. When the computer plays video or audio it is reading this information in the media files and turning it into a video or audio signal that plays on the monitor or from the speakers. These files, particularly the video files, can be extremely large. One minute of video using certain HD codecs, for instance, takes up almost 1 gigabyte (over 1 billion bytes, or 8 billion bits of information) of space on a computer hard drive. For this reason, the hard drives that hold the media files must be large.

The computer editing system creates a **clip** for every media file. A clip is essentially a set of directions that tell the computer where the media file is located and which portion of the file to play. When a clip is edited, all that is changed is the set of directions in the clip describing how to play the media file; the media file itself remains unchanged. If the end of a clip is shortened, for instance, that media is still part of the media file but is no longer played when the clip is played.

Clips, unlike the media files they refer to, are very small files, on the order of several kilobytes (thousands of bytes). The clips are separate from the media files. If the media files are erased, the clips remain in the project file. These clips now refer to missing files and are called **off-line clips**. Since the clips include directions for everything that has been done to the media files, restoring the media files by re-capturing them restores all of the editing actions done to them, possibly saving many hours of work. If the clips are deleted from the project file, the media files they refer to may remain on the media drives, but the project file has no way to gain access to them. In that case, if there is no backup of the project file, it will be necessary to re-edit the entire project. Most editing programs, though, automatically back up the project files at regular intervals. When a media drive is nearly full, deleting unwanted clips will not free up much space. The unwanted media files that these clips point to must be deleted as well.

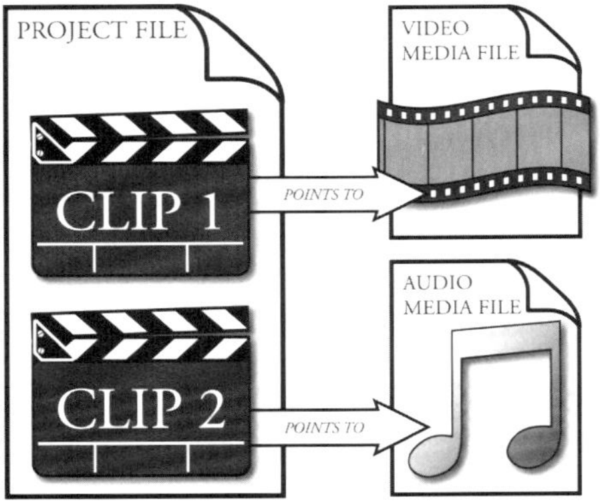

In non-linear editing systems, the actual video and audio files are not part of the project file. Instead the project file uses clips as pointers to the media files.

Editing on a computer is usually referred to as **non-destructive editing**. If the editor decides to restore a clip to its original length, the media file does not need to be recaptured; the clip is simply modified so that more of the media file is played. The connection between clips and media files is the heart of computerized editing systems and gives an editor enormous freedom to try various edits, make multiple versions of the same project and experiment with different ideas. Because almost any action can be undone easily, the cost of experimentation is relatively low, and the editing scheme can be based on aesthetic and creative factors rather than technical limitations.

The interface of a non-linear system is the collection of on-screen windows and buttons that allow the editor to manipulate video and audio. Though every system's interface is different in the details, in general they are similar and are usually based upon the design of a linear editing system. There is a "bin" or "browser window" that stores the clips available to be edited, a source window in which incoming video is previewed, a record-monitor window that shows the edited video and a **timeline** that shows the final sequence of the video and audio clips in the edited piece.

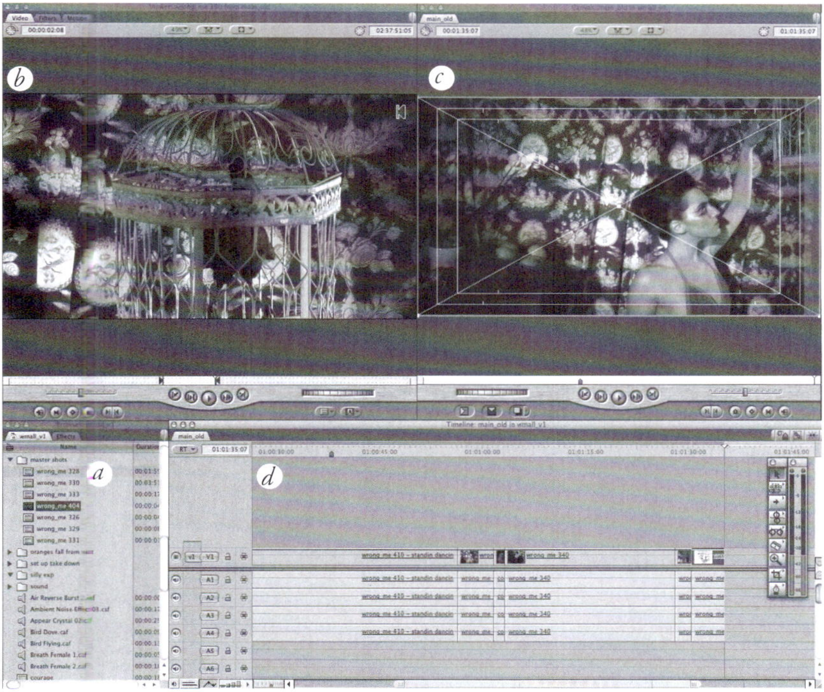

A typical non-linear editing interface, showing a) the browser window; b) the source window; c) the record-monitor window; d) the timeline.

The timeline consists of multiple video and audio **tracks**. A track is a visual representation of video or audio clips, showing their order and length in the edited sequence. Blocks that represent the edited clips are laid end-to-end on each track of the timeline. A clip that appears to the right of another clip is played after that clip; the point at which two clips touch represents the cut or transition from one clip to the next. A clip that appears directly above or below another clip plays simultaneously with that clip; if a music clip on an audio track is below a close-up on a video track, the music will play when the close-up is seen. Using multiple tracks of audio allows several sounds to play at once, creating a layered, complex soundtrack. Using several tracks of video allows the editor to create complex visual effects like superimpositions and **composite shots** that combine elements of several shots into one image. For instance, a simple composite shot might combine a shot of an actor with a previously recorded shot of a volcano, making it appear as though the actor is in the exotic location.

The process of editing on a non-linear system usually involves viewing clips and editing pieces of them into the timeline in the desired order until a rough cut is completed. At this point all of the clips are in the timeline in the proper order, but the lengths of the clips and the edit points between them may need some adjustment. This is where the strength of non-linear editing shows most clearly. Clips can be trimmed frame by frame, and manipulating video and audio clips is nearly as simple as manipulating text in a word-processing program. Clips can be cut, pasted, duplicated or shifted to any position in the timeline with a keystroke or a click of the mouse. If a particular operation turns out to be a mistake, the "Undo" key can usually avert disaster.

Another advantage of non-linear editing is that most systems allow for a multitude of audio tracks. This makes it very easy to create an overall soundtrack that is the result of many layers of sound. Rather than trying to record all sounds on the set, the production crew can concentrate on getting clear, "clean" dialogue without any background sound. The editor can then add sounds that make the scene seem more realistic and interesting.

Music can be added as well, either as a kind of ambient sound to cover audio edits or to create a mood or trigger an emotional response in the viewer. Audio tracks can be used to add **sound effects**, sounds that are created by objects or people in the movie. Footsteps, the sound of a car driving by or the crash of a glass falling to the floor are all examples of sound effects that are tied to specific actions or events on screen. By creating and editing these tracks of dialogue, music, sound effects and ambient sound, the filmmaker can design a rich, densely layered sound environment that works with the visual track to engage the audience more fully in the experience of the film.

Digital editing also makes it very easy to manipulate the video image itself. Since the digital video image is a series of numbers, and computers manipulate numbers very well, the image can be changed in ways that would have been difficult if not impossible in film or analog video. These changes can be basic, like subtly changing the color of a shot so that it matches other shots in the same scene. The changes can be extreme, like combining live-action video with a computer-generated background to create a shot that could not be constructed in the real world.

This allows an editor to create a large array of video effects. The most common kinds of video effects are **filters** that change the color, brightness or other characteristics of the video signal, **motion effects** in which the size, shape or frame of the video image is moved, rotated or distorted in some way and composite shots in which two or more video images are combined to create a new image.

When an editor first places a filter on a video clip, creates a motion effect or adds two or more layers of video together, the editing system creates a set of instructions detailing how to manipulate the video. Based on these instructions the system adds the two shots together or adds the video and filter together in order to produce a preview of the effect. Since this procedure can take a lot of processing power and time, most such previews can only be constructed one frame at a time, and in order to preview the effect the editor must step through the footage very slowly. Enabling the effect to be played back at the proper speed (or in "real time") requires the computer to create a **render file**.

The render file is a new media file that incorporates the desired effect. For instance, when a composite shot is rendered, the computer blends the two images together frame by frame to create an entirely new media file. Depending on the effect and the configuration of the computer, rendering may take several seconds or several hours. When it is finished and the composite shot is played, it is the newly created render file that plays, not either of the original video clips. Since this render file contains frames that already combine both images, no actual blending is required, and the composite shot can be played back as easily as any other shot. Of course, render files take up as much space as other media files, and storage space must be available for these new files.

After the video and audio have been captured, edited and combined with titles and other graphic elements, and effects and filters have been added and rendered, the video is ready to be transferred out of the computer to its final exhibition and distribution format. The three general ways to output video from the computer are to print to video, to create an EDL for on-line editing or to export as a digital file.

Printing to video is the opposite of capturing from videotape. After the sequence has been edited and all effects and transitions have been rendered, the final video and audio information can be sent out of the computer to a video deck. The deck is put into record mode and the edited sequence is played. The video and audio information travels to the deck which lays the information down on the videotape. This tape is the editing master that is used to make dubs for distribution.

The process of creating an EDL from a non-linear system is very similar to that using a linear off-line editing system. One potential pitfall, however, is that if you are moving to a videotape-based on-line editing suite, it cannot recreate the range of effects and functions possible in a non-linear system. An editor moving from a non-linear off-line system to a linear on-line system should resist using the full range of 3-D transitions, multiple video layers and computer-aided effects that are within the capabilities of the non-linear system. Using these effects may result in an EDL that an on-line editor cannot use. Of course, if the on-line edit is done on a non-linear system, the full range of functions and effects will be available.

Finally, the edited sequence can be saved as a digital file for use on the internet, mobile devices, Blu-ray or DVD. These options, along with other exhibition and distribution issues, are discussed in Chapter 12, *Distribution*.

Film-to-Video Transfer

The previous section describes the process of non-linear editing for projects shot on video. Most movies that are shot on film are also edited digitally. To make this possible the film must first be transferred to video, either on tape or as a digital file.

The least expensive method of transferring film to tape is to use a video camera to shoot the film while it is being projected onto a small screen. In a dark room, project the film onto a smooth, non-glaring white surface (copier paper works well). Keep the projected image small so it will be as sharp as possible. Position a video camera on a tripod as close to the projector as possible and make sure both projector and camera are focused properly before taping. Using this technique the quality of the transfer will depend on the type of projector used, the quality of the video camera and the video format. Regardless of the format and the equipment used, this method will not yield the highest quality results.

Many photographic supply stores and certain film labs offer an inexpensive film-to-video transfer service. They will almost always transfer film to video using a **film chain**. A film chain uses a video camera and a film projector with a mirror set at a 45-degree angle between them. The mirror directs the projected image into the lens of the camera as the footage is recorded on video. The iris of the video camera is usually fixed at a single setting, so variations in exposure on the film cannot be corrected. Alternately, as the brightness of the film image changes, the iris of the video camera can be adjusted "on the fly," but this results in momentary problems with exposure. Again the quality of the transfer will depend on the video format and the projector and the camera equipment used.

By far, the best results are achieved with a **telecine** or **datacine** system, a more sophisticated electronic transfer. This type of video transfer is much more expensive than a film chain transfer, but it is the only system that provides the opportunity to manipulate the color, contrast and brightness of individual shots as they will appear on tape. It is also the only system capable of making a transfer that creates and maintains a precise relationship between film frames and video frames. Most professional motion picture laboratories offer electronic transfer of film to videotape (telecine) or digital file (datacine).

Editing Film Digitally for Video Release

Filmmakers often shoot on film rather than video to get the "look" of film, whether for the high resolution, large tonal range and vivid colors of color negative or the grainy, dramatic, high-contrast images of black-and-white reversal film. Once the film has been shot it is transferred to video, edited digitally and released on video. In this case, once the film has been transferred to video, the process of editing is exactly the same as it is for editing video, and the full range of effects and output options are available to the editor. When planning to release the film on video, the film footage should be transferred at the highest possible quality. Since the video created by the telecine or datacine transfer will serve as the original master material for editing purposes, it is critical that this footage looks as good as it can. Of course, if there are problems with a portion of the transferred material, it is always possible to transfer that portion again from the original film footage.

Editing Film Digitally for Film Release

Many films, particularly feature-length films, are made by shooting on film, editing digitally and then conforming the film negative to match the digital edit in order to create a final print on film. When working in this way the edited version is used as a sort of "digital workprint" that guides the conforming process. A filmmaker working in this manner usually requests **video dailies** from the film laboratory instead of, or in addition to, a film workprint or high-quality video transfer. Video dailies are a special type of film-to-video transfer that can be made more quickly and inexpensively, with less attention to color and exposure correction. Like a film workprint, video dailies are a rough copy of the original camera footage to be used solely for editing purposes. Video dailies must contain special frame identification information that ordinary film-to-video transfers do not contain.

As explained earlier, each roll of 16mm and 35mm film has identifying numbers, latent edge numbers, printed on the edge of the camera original footage. The footage also has a machine-readable bar code version of that edge numbering, called keycode, along its edge. Each video frame is assigned a number using **SMPTE timecode**. SMPTE (Society of Motion Picture and Television Engineers) timecode uses a specific number for every frame on a tape so that video editing can be frame-exact. These video timecode numbers are different from the latent edge numbers and keycode found on the camera original film footage.

The video dailies should include both timecode and keycode information. In the transfer process the timecode and the keycode numbers can be made visible in a window on every frame of the transferred video. It is critical when the transfer is made that the keycode information is precisely accurate. After editing is complete this information will be used to conform the original camera footage to the computer edit, a process known as **matchback**. The matchback process involves cross-referencing timecode and keycode information so that every digital edit can be matched to the correct film frames for physical cutting. Some computerized editing systems have built-in capabilities to match timecode and keycode so that matchback will be accurate.

If the film is transferred to NTSC videotape that runs at 29.97fps, the transfer must also compensate for the difference between this frame rate and film's 24fps frame rate. In order to compensate for the difference in frame rate, film shot at 24fps is transferred to videotape using a method called **pulldown**. Pulldown is a transfer method in which film frames are copied onto multiple video fields in order to make the running time of the images on the videotape precisely match the running time of the images on the film being copied. Ten seconds of video must correspond to exactly ten seconds of film. The most common method of converting film to video is **2:3 pulldown**. This process recognizes and takes advantage of the fact that each interlaced video frame is divided into two fields. Using the 2:3 pulldown transfer method, the first film frame is recorded onto two fields (1 video frame). The next film frame is recorded onto three fields (1.5 video frames). The next film frame is recorded onto two fields, and the following film frame is recorded onto three fields. This process converts four film frames into five video frames, changing the frame rate from the film's 24fps to 30fps on videotape. Since NTSC video actually runs at exactly 29.97fps (0.1% slower than 30fps), the film is also slowed down by 0.1% to 23.976fps during the transfer. The 2:3 pulldown in combination with this 0.1% slowdown converts 24 frames per second film to video running at 29.97 frames per second.

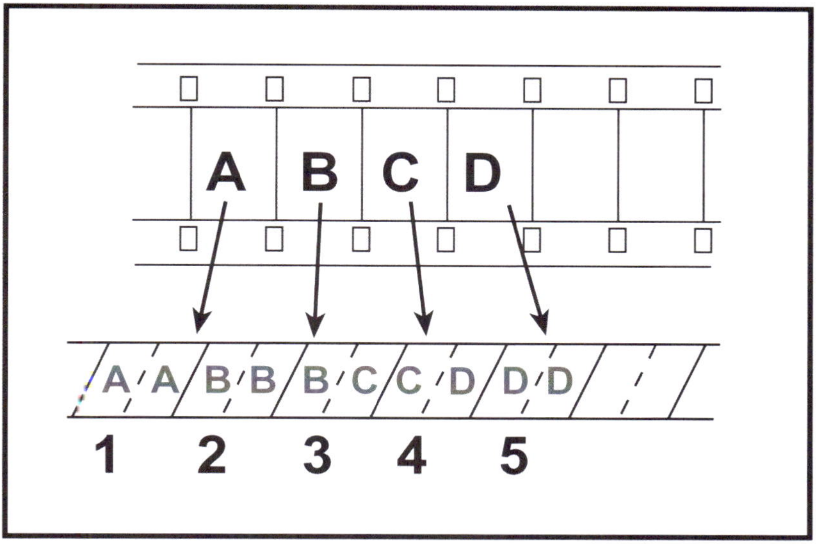

2:3 pulldown. Four film frames are converted to five video frames. Frames A and C transfer to 2 video fields. Frames B and D are transferred to 3 video fields.

If the transfer was made at the standard NTSC video frame rate of 29.97fps, before editing begins it can be converted back to the film's transfer rate of 23.976fps in most editing systems through a process called **reverse telecine**. Reverse telecine discards the extra video fields that are created during the 2:3 pulldown process and establishes a one-video-frame-to-one-film-frame relationship. Of course, if you transfer to an HD file rather than an NTSC videotape, you have the option of transferring to video that runs at 24fps, making a 2:3 pulldown and reverse telecine unnecessary. Often, though, the film transport in the datacine at the film lab might still run at 23.976fps, and the video file will have an actual frame rate of 23.976fps. In this case (as in the case of a 2:3 pulldown) audio recorded in synchronization with the film will also have to be slowed down by 0.1% in order to stay in sync with the slowed down video.

It is always important to talk to the film lab before starting a project, since different labs may use different methods and formats for transfers that will ultimately go through the matchback process. Generally, the transfer from film should be made with both keycode and timecode visible, burnt into the image. Usually, the lab will provide a file that contains all of the keycode and timecode information (beginning and ending keycode and timecode numbers) for each shot that was transferred. There are a number of standard file formats, such as Flexfile, that are commonly used, depending on the non-linear editing system that will be employed.

Once the video and audio has been synchronized in the computer, the editing process is very similar to editing for video release, but with certain limitations. When editing material that has been transferred from film and which will ultimately be finished as a film print, it is important to remember that the film print will be made from the negative (or reversal original) that ran through the camera and which was used to make the transfer to a digital format. The negative doesn't include any graphics or effects that might have been added in the non-linear editing system. A film lab can easily add fades or dissolves when making a print, as long as the printing original has been prepared properly, but standard lengths for these effects (16, 24, 32, 48, 64 or 96 frames) must be used. Odd lengths for such effects or specialized graphics (such as a wipe or a title over the picture) can only be achieved if a piece of negative that incorporates the effect is made first.

Making a new piece of film negative with built-in effects can be done in two ways. The elements can be combined on film using an optical printer, or the film elements can be scanned (at a film lab using specialized equipment) at high resolution to make new digital files. These digital files can be combined to create the desired effect and then the new composite image can be scanned back to film, again at high resolution using a specialized scanner. This scanning process is very expensive. It is also important to remember that, while it's easy to repeat the same shot many times in a non-linear system, only one piece of negative exists for each shot.

When editing is complete the edit consists of a series of clips on a timeline. Those clips have in and out points that are defined by timecode numbers. In order to cut the film negative accurately the timecode numbers need to be translated to match the corresponding keycode numbers on the original film. These keycode numbers are compiled into a cut list that is then used to cut the exact frames needed for conforming the negative. Conforming is usually done by a specialist at the film lab where the answer print will be made. In order to make the answer print the lab will also need audio files or a mixed audio track. If the project was edited at 23.976fps, the audio will need to be sped up by 0.1% since the answer print will be projected at 24fps.

Titles, Transitions and Graphics

Before the video is complete titles, transitions and graphics can be added. Most editing software has the capability to create simple titles such as **lower thirds** that show an interview subject's name near the bottom of the screen or ending credits that scroll up the screen. Specialty software can create elaborate animated titles that can be imported into the project.

Transitions define what happens at the edit point between shots. The simplest transition from one shot to another is the cut, created when clips are placed beside each other on the timeline. Fades, dissolves and other more elaborate transitions are possible. A **fade-in** is a transition in which a blank (usually black) screen gradually reveals an image until that image is fully realized on screen and is often used to begin a scene. A **fade-out** is a transition in which a shot at full value gradually diminishes to a black screen. Fade-outs often occur at the end of a scene and are generally used to suggest a passage of time. A **dissolve** is a transition in which it appears as if one image blends into another image. A dissolve is actually a fade-out superimposed with a fade-in. In a **wipe** one shot replaces the other by replacing a small piece of the image area of the screen and taking over more and more of the frame until the outgoing shot is completely gone. Wipes, split screens and dozens of filters that can alter the video image in a variety of ways are among the available options. Often, the easy access to so many flashy options can be a distraction that leads beginners to over-use effects, ultimately to the detriment of the project.

When creating graphics for use in a video, it is important to remember that colors, movement and even aspect ratios can look very different on a video monitor than on a computer monitor. Most graphics programs, such as Adobe Photoshop, have a variety of presets and templates for matching standard-definition and high-definition video specifications. Even so, if you are editing a video project from beginning to end on a computer monitor you may be surprised at how different it looks on a video monitor. If your project is meant to be viewed on a television, make sure you check it on a television before you output it.

Archiving and Storage

Motion picture film will last for many years if it is stored properly. There are a few important guidelines to follow. Tape down the end of the leader so that the film will not unravel or become loose on the reel. Never pull on the end of a loose roll of film to tighten it, since this can result in "cinch marks." Cinching is a type of scratching that occurs when one layer of film rubs against another, and pulling on the end of a roll of film can create cinch marks throughout the entire roll. Store the reel of film in a plastic or metal can or some other light-tight, dust-free container. For long-term storage plastic reels and cans are preferable to metal ones. Films should always be stored in dark, cool, dry places. Avoid hot attics, wet basements or other areas that might subject a film to extremes of heat or humidity.

Video is a more volatile medium. The aim of creating "archival" copies of your video is to preserve the digital data so that it can be retrieved and updated as old formats disappear and new ones arise. You'll need to create and output a full-quality copy of your finished work and store it on something that will still be playable a few years from now. You could print to videotape of the same format used to shoot the original footage, as long as you're sure that you'll have access to a camera or deck that will play that tape when you need to make a new copy. You could make a full-quality digital file and store it on a hard drive or copy it to a DVD-ROM or a data Blu-ray disc. For backup purposes you might do both.

Chapter 9

Pre-Production

The filmmaking process is divided into three phases: pre-production (the planning of the film), production (the actual shooting) and post-production (editing and laboratory work). In many ways the pre-production phase is the most important of the three. When the making of a film is properly planned the shooting and editing will be less hectic and more efficient.

Writing the Film

A film begins as an idea. While initially a film might grow out of a simple concept, the basic idea is often developed into a more and more complex construction. When describing an idea for a film a filmmaker might write a **proposal** that explains what the film is about and what kind of a film it is going to be. This proposal might be written for a potential funder, for a filmmaking teacher or simply for the purpose of clarifying the film's concept. The proposal can be as short as two or three paragraphs describing the subject matter, the basic idea and the stylistic approach to the material.

After a proposal is written the film's concept must be combined with the structure which best fits that concept. In a film **treatment** the idea is described in more specific terms. The written treatment concentrates on the film's structure and the most effective presentation of the material. A treatment for a documentary or an experimental film might emphasize the filmmaker's point of view or approach to the material. If it is a narrative film it usually includes a general description of each character in the film as well as a short statement outlining the filmmaker's intent. A narrative treatment usually presents the plot scene by scene but not shot by shot. It describes the important events that advance the plot within each scene. A treatment for *Citizen Kane* might begin like this:

Scene 1. **The Mansion of the wealthy Charles Foster Kane. Kane, old and bedridden, dies. His last word is "Rosebud."**

Scene 2. **A newsreel summarizing the important events of Kane's life. These events will be shown in greater detail and from a more personal perspective later.**

Scene 3. **A screening room. Unhappy with the newsreel, the newsreel producer orders a reporter to find out what "Rosebud" means.**

And so on for every scene in the film. Dialogue and details of actions are not included in a film treatment. At this point all that is important are the twists of the plot. The treatment describes concisely what happens in the film and the order in which events unfold.

A filmmaker would not begin to shoot with just a treatment. When making a narrative film the next step is writing a more detailed **script** or **screenplay**. The script contains all of the scenes from the treatment. Each scene is written to include all of the relevant action and dialogue. Scripts are also written in a specialized format so that certain kinds of information, most of it necessary for planning and scheduling, can be found easily. A properly formatted scene in a script might look like this:

4. INT. BEDROOM NIGHT.

JUSTIN is sitting on the edge of the bed watching as PAIGE packs her clothes into an old suitcase.

JUSTIN
You're leaving then?

PAIGE
I can't believe you neutered Scott.

Paige finishes packing and walks out of the room. Justin remains seated on the bed. The front door SLAMS.

5. EXT. HOUSE - NIGHT
Paige walks away from the house carrying her suitcase. It begins to RAIN.

And so on for every scene in the film. Several aspects of the format are worth a closer look. Each scene is numbered, making it easy to identify and refer to individual scenes during the planning stage as well as during the shooting and the editing of the film. After each scene number the scene is designated as an interior ("INT") or an exterior ("EXT") location. This helps in planning the shooting schedule. After the "INT" or "EXT" designation the location is given, followed by the notation "DAY" or "NIGHT." This top line provides most of the important information about the scene needed for scheduling: whether it takes place inside or outside, where it takes place and at what time of day it's supposed to occur. The first time a character's name appears in the script, it is typed in capital letters. After that it is written normally within the body of the script. When a character is speaking, the character's name is always typed in capitals and it is centered on the page, setting it apart from the body of the script. The character's dialogue is centered under the name. These aspects of the format allow a reader to skim through the script to see how many different characters appear in the film or to look at an individual scene and quickly identify which characters have speaking parts. Any sound effects that are described in the script are capitalized. This sort of information is useful in planning and scheduling for production.

A script does *not* include shot descriptions, camera angles or directions for camera movement. The script is for other people (actors, crew, funders and so on) to read, and it is too time consuming and distracting to get through a long script with all of the shooting details included. After the script has described what will happen in front of the camera, the director decides where the camera will be placed, what types of shots will be used and how they will be composed. This information is detailed in a **shooting script** and also in a **storyboard**.

The shooting script describes every shot, every camera angle and every movement for each scene in the script. Since the shooting script is mainly for the use of the director and the cinematographer, format isn't as important as it is in the script. A shooting script for the scene previously described in script form might look like this:

4. INT. BEDROOM NIGHT

1. **LS bedroom. Justin is sitting on the bed watching Paige pack.**
2. **MCU Justin looking at Paige.**
3. **MS Paige packing.**
4. **CU Justin: "You're leaving then?"**
5. **CU Paige: "I can't believe you neutered Scott."**
6. **CU Scott dazed.**
7. **MS Paige finishes packing. PAN with her as she walks out the door. Continue PAN from door to MS Justin. The front door SLAMS**

One problem with scripts and shooting scripts is that they are written descriptions of visual images. In a storyboard the filmmaker sketches a frame to represent each shot in the shooting script. This enables the filmmaker to visualize what the shots will look like rather than relying on a written description of them. The storyboard also provides greater detail. For instance, "MS Justin" could look like this:

or it might look like this:

A storyboard is similar to a comic strip version of a film and, in fact, comic book artists often work as professional storyboardists. However, since a storyboard's main purpose is to serve as an aid in planning a shoot, it does not need to be slick and well drawn. What is important is that the overall spatial relationships, image sizes and screen directions are clear from the drawings. Even if your drawings are simple stick figures, you can create a useful storyboard that shows proportionate image sizes, camera angles and the direction people are facing in each shot. Consider the following storyboard based on the shooting script on page 131:

1. LS Bedroom.
Justin watches as Paige packs.

2. MCU Justin.

3. MS Paige packing.

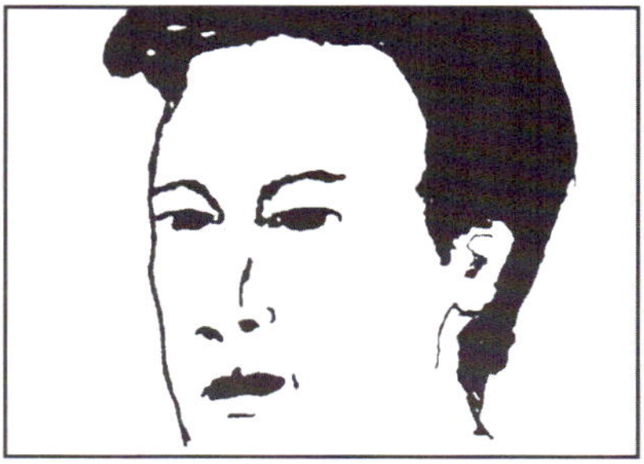

4. CU Justin "You're leaving then?"

5. CU Paige "I can't believe you neutered Scott!"

6. CU Scott, dazed.

7a.

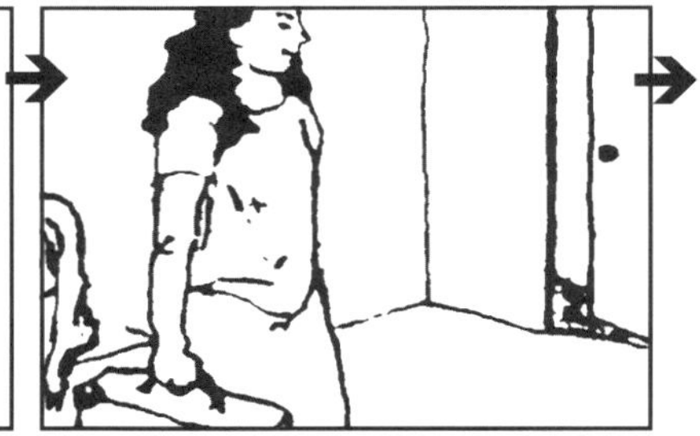

7b.

7c.

MS Paige finishes packing. PAN as Paige moves to door. Continue PAN to MS Justin sitting on bed.

Some films do not require all of the scripting phases that have been outlined. A very short film might go straight from treatment to storyboard to production, skipping over the script and the shooting script. It might be impossible to create a detailed treatment for some documentary films. The nature of most documentary films is that the actions that occur in front of the camera cannot be predicted. Certain experimental films and some kinds of documentaries can be approached in a more freehand way, without knowing ahead of time exactly what you want. Writing treatments and scripts for such productions can still be quite useful though. A written description of what the film *might* be can help the filmmaker to imagine and anticipate situations and can provide the filmmaker with a potential structure, so the approach to the material will not be random. In such cases production can become a process of exploration and discovery. This approach can require a lot more money, time and effort to create a unified finished piece out of what was shot at the spur of the moment, and it can involve a lot of risk, but the rewards can be great too. Generally, the less work you do in pre-production, the more work you will have to do in post-production to make a film succeed. In many cases the lack of proper pre-production creates an insurmountable obstacle to the creation of a successful film.

Preparations

Depending on the length, scope and specific details of your project, you are likely to need more than just a camera to shoot it. Even small projects usually require some sort of technical crew during production. The crew might be as small as two or three people, or a crew can be quite large. It is important to form an appropriate crew during pre-production. You will need to find people with the right kind of expertise (camera, sound, lighting and so on) with whom you will be able to work and communicate. You will also need to find people who are willing and able to commit the time it will take to get the film done. If the film calls for actors, you will need to find people who can perform in the way that you want them to, but at the same time, you'll want to be sure that you are choosing reliable people who will show up on time and stick with the project. In choosing an actor it may be more important to find someone you can work with and whose schedule is flexible than it is to find a trained actor whose availability may be limited. However, it is most important that the actors you choose fit their roles. If the story is about a jaded hit man you don't want to use a 20-year-old friend to play the part.

Scouting locations is another important part of pre-production. The locations you choose should be visually interesting and should fit the scenes. If the film's central character is wealthy, don't use a dorm room to depict the study in his mansion. Accessibility is crucial in choosing a location. Be sure to obtain the necessary permission to shoot, and not just once. You should always establish a backup date in case an actor or crew member backs out, the weather is uncooperative or shooting takes longer than anticipated. Finally, make sure adequate electrical power is available to accommodate the shoot's lighting needs.

The film might also require specific props and costumes. Again it is important that these items fit the scene. For instance, the wealthy character shouldn't be driving around in a beat-up old car. Many of the decisions made during pre-production will affect the **production value** of the film. Production value is determined by those elements that contribute to the look of the film and make it more convincing. Locations, sets, costumes, props and actors, as well as technical considerations such as lighting and camera work all contribute to the overall quality and believability of the film's look, or the production value of the film. Coordinating all these elements may seem overwhelming, but with adequate preparation high production value can be achieved without getting terribly elaborate.

Scheduling is also a crucial part of pre-production. If the film is large, scheduling can be a major job of coordinating the availability of technical crew, actors, locations and equipment. For a small film it can be much simpler, but it is no less important. A **script breakdown** enables a filmmaker to more easily organize a list of locations, actors, props, costumes and any other details necessary for the film. A script breakdown helps in scheduling the shooting of the film in the most logical way. The breakdown makes it easy to see information such as which actors and props are needed at each location and which portions of the script will be shot at each location. The script breakdown can also give the filmmaker an idea of how many days each location will be needed. A simple script breakdown for the film about Justin and Paige might look like this:

Script Breakdown:

Scene	Page	Location	Actors	Costumes/Props	Misc.
1	1,2,3	Justin & Paige's Bedroom	Justin, Paige Scott	Pajamas, Coffee Cups	Cat Wrangler
2	4,5,6	Charlie's Diner	Justin, Paige, Gus, Zoey	Plates with Food	8-10 Extras
3	7	Exterior Dr. Schnitt's Office	Justin, Scott	Justin's Car Justin's Jacket Scott's Leash	Cat Wrangler
4	8	Justin & Paige's Bedroom	Justin, Paige Scott	Suitcase, Clothes Paige's Coat	Cat Wrangler
5	9	Exterior House	Paige	Suitcase, Paige's Coat	Fake Rain

It is a good idea to schedule rehearsal time prior to shooting for narrative films, and it is always important to schedule backup dates for shooting regardless of the type of film you are making. Keep in mind that things usually take longer than expected. Beyond that, there are so many variables involved in making a film that something unpredictable can happen to slow a shoot down or to cause a cancellation. Prepare for the unexpected by making contingency plans ahead of time.

Final Planning

When you visit a location, it is a good idea to sketch a rough floor plan of the space. You can use this to create a **shooting plan** for each location. While the shooting script gives the order of shots as they are intended to appear *in the edited film*, the shooting plan arranges the shots in the order that you would actually shoot them. It is almost always faster and more economical to shoot out of sequence. In the example of the scene involving Paige and Justin, you wouldn't light and shoot the medium close-up of Justin (shot 2), move the camera and the lights to shoot Paige's medium shot (shot 3) and then move it all back again to light and shoot Justin's next close-up (shot 4). Instead, once you've set up a camera position and done the lighting for that set-up, it makes much more sense to shoot all the shots that are called for (in the shooting script or storyboard) from that particular camera angle. By doing this you can capture the seven shots in the shooting script (and in the storyboard) with only four camera set-ups. A shooting plan for the shooting script on page 131 might look like this:

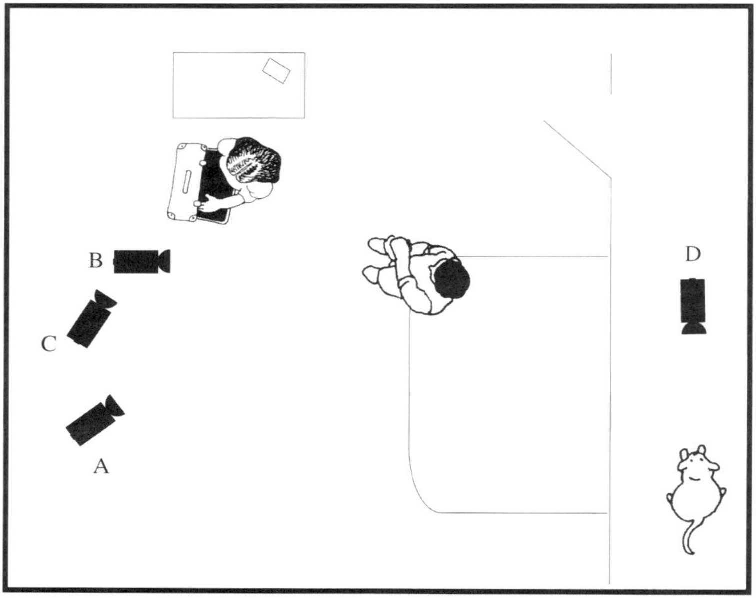

Camera position A, in the corner of the room, captures the establishing shot (shot 1). By changing to a longer lens setting, you can shoot shot 7 (the pan) from the same position. Position B covers shots 2 and 4, the shots of Justin alone. Position C captures the shots of Paige (shots 3 and 5). Camera position D, the close-up of the cat, is put aside out of the shooting plan to indicate that, if necessary, it can be shot anywhere at any time.

Lighting diagrams can also be helpful when planning the details of a shoot. Good lighting diagrams made ahead of time can save time on the day of the shoot and can also assist in planning for the lighting equipment that will be needed. Each camera position defined in the shooting plan is likely to require a separate lighting diagram. The lighting diagrams simply indicate where, tentatively, the lights should be placed for each camera set-up. Undoubtedly, some changes or fine-tuning will be necessary when actually lighting the location, but lighting diagrams speed things up by providing a well-considered starting point. A lighting diagram for the camera position that will cover shots 3 and 5 in the bedroom scene might look like this:

A lighting diagram for one camera position from the shooting plan on page 138.

In a scene this simple, it might be hard to see just how economical shooting out of sequence can be. The more complex the film, the more time and effort that can be saved. For instance, if the lighting is very complicated it can take hours to light a shot, and every change in the camera set-up usually requires a change in the lighting. Reducing seven shots to only four set-ups might save several hours. Also, if the shoot will take all day and the actors are available for only a few hours each, you can arrange it so that all the shots involving only Justin are shot first, allowing Paige to arrive on the set later. If you then shoot all of the shots involving both characters, you can let Justin go early and finish the day with Paige's close-ups. (Of course, it is preferable to have both actors present for the entire shoot, if possible.)

While the preparations discussed here refer primarily to narrative filmmaking, planning is important for documentaries as well. If you are familiar with the location, you can determine which camera angles will work best and how you might break the space down into various shots. If people will appear in the film, talk to them and let them get comfortable with you before you show up to shoot, since a camera can make people uncomfortable and self-conscious. Be certain that everyone who will appear in the film wants to participate and gives you permission to shoot them.

Finally, when making a film on a limited budget, one way to begin pre-production is to consider the resources available and to utilize them in planning the film. If you happen to have access to an interesting location, consider adapting a scene or an action to fit that location. If a friend has a particular talent, you might find a way to incorporate it into the film.

The purpose of thorough pre-production is to maximize the chances of completing a well-realized film, to avoid wasting the time of the people who are assisting you and to get through the shooting with some shred of sanity. If everything is planned in as much detail as possible before shooting, you won't have to spend so much time worrying that you are missing a necessary shot. Some of the inevitable confusion is avoided, allowing more time for creative thinking on the set.

Chapter 10

Lighting

It is usually necessary to supplement, modify or invent lighting conditions when shooting a subject on film or video. Many beginners believe that one advantage of shooting video is that supplemental lighting is usually unnecessary. This misconception has arisen because in many situations a video camera can record some sort of image using existing light. In most interior situations and frequently when shooting exteriors the natural or available light is insufficient in either its quantity or its quality to produce images that will create the exposure level and the mood required of a particular scene. Neither film nor video interprets light in the same way the human eye and brain do. For these reasons it is necessary for beginning filmmakers to know as much as possible about the characteristics and uses of light.

Light has four basic characteristics: angle, quality, color and intensity. Controlling these characteristics carefully will create images that enhance mood or guide emotion, clarify meaning or lead the viewer's eye to significant details in the shot.

Lighting Angles

A light source will create different effects on the subject depending upon the angle of its placement. Vertical lighting angles refer to the height of the light, and horizontal angles refer to the light's position around the subject. In terms of height, lighting from above seems most natural and most pleasing, because in life almost all light comes from overhead. Light from the sun comes from above, and we are accustomed to seeing most things lit from a high vertical angle.

Frontal lighting.

45° lighting.

Side lighting.

Three-quarter back lighting.

Back lighting.

Lighting from below, on the other hand, looks unnatural. When a person's face is lit from underneath, areas that would normally be in shadow, such as the underside of the chin and the tops of the eye sockets, are illuminated. Shadows fall upward rather than downward. Lighting from below is often used to create an eerie atmosphere or to make a character or setting seem dangerous or unnatural. *Touch of Evil* (1959) Orson Welles' "B-movie" masterpiece, makes good use of lighting from below in depicting unscrupulous characters and dangerous situations.

Since lights are usually positioned somewhere above eye level, the horizontal angle of a light source is often a filmmaker's primary consideration in lighting a scene (see examples on p. 143). Head-on frontal lighting produces a flat, unattractive look, much like snapshots taken with only a flash for illumination. Light that hits the subject from a 45-degree angle produces "classic" modeling. The nose shadow falls to the side and a little below the nose, and the eye sockets are not filled with shadow. Side lighting (at a 90-degree angle to the camera/subject axis) produces a very dramatic image. There is contrast between the light and dark sides of the face, and the face seems to be cut in half by the light. Three-quarter back light makes a subject look mysterious; most of the face is covered in shadow, with light striking the temple or the edge of the cheek. In the same way back lighting, from almost directly behind, can lend a subject mystery and power; the subject is outlined by a halo of light.

Quality of Light

Discussions of the quality of a light source center on the type of lighting effect it creates. A **hard** light source produces parallel light rays that hit an object from a single angle. When hard light strikes an object it creates hard-edged, well-defined shadows. Sunlight on a clear, cloudless day is an example of hard light. Since hard light creates hard shadows it emphasizes the texture of the objects that it hits. If a person's face is illuminated by a hard light source, every whisker, blemish and scar will cast a distinct shadow and will tend to stand out. In old westerns heroes like John Wayne and Clint Eastwood looked tough and rugged thanks to hard light sources.

Soft light is the result of many rays of light striking the subject from many different angles. Soft light tends to wrap around an object, casting less distinct shadows, de-emphasizing texture and smoothing over blemishes. Sunlight on a cloudy day is a good example of soft light, since the parallel light rays of the sun are diffused (or scattered) by the clouds. Shadows on the ground are indistinct and soft-edged. In old Hollywood films actors were often lit with soft light to smooth out blemishes or wrinkles and to make them appear younger and more attractive.

A lighting unit designed as a hard light source can also be used to create soft light. A hard light can be bounced off a white surface and the resulting light will be quite soft. It is common practice to bounce lights from the walls or ceiling of a room. If the walls aren't white or if they are too far away from the subject being lit, a large piece of white foam core (available at most art supply stores) makes a good, portable **bounce card**. A lighting unit known as a "softlight" can also be used. A softlight is a specialized instrument that incorporates a large silvered reflector and one or two high-wattage lamps that shine directly into it, bouncing the light and producing a very bright and very soft light source. Hard light sources can also be softened to a lesser extent by placing diffusion material in front of the light. **Diffusion**, a gauze-like, heat-resistant material that is available in a number of styles, scatters rays of light as they pass through it.

Color

The color of daylight is bluer than that of tungsten light (see Chapter 2, *The Film Camera and Film Stock*). When shooting video or color film a filmmaker must be careful about mixing daylight and tungsten light sources. If bright daylight coming through a window is used as the brightest light in a shot of a person, and tungsten-balanced light is used to fill in the shadows, there will be two different colors of light on the subject's face. In most situations this is not a desirable effect, especially when lighting a human face. If the tungsten light is intended to appear to be just the ambient light in the room, and the scene is meant to look natural and unlit, then the difference in colors will defeat this aim. Usually either the daylight source (the window) or the tungsten-balanced source must be filtered so that both sources are creating the same color of light.

In order to match the tungsten-balanced fill light with the daylight coming through the window, a **full blue** (or **daylight blue**) **gel** could be placed in front of the tungsten light source. A gel is a sheet of acetate material used to filter light. The tungsten-balanced light passing through the blue gel is converted to the color of the daylight coming through the window. In terms of color it is as if all the light in the scene is daylight. In this situation daylight-balanced film will not require any filtration. If you are shooting tungsten-balanced film, place an orange filter (85 filter) in front of the lens so that all the light that hits the film will be properly filtered to match the tungsten-balanced film. If you are shooting video, you can set the white balance to its daylight preset or white balance the camera manually once the overall lighting has been established.

Alternately, you could place an **orange 85 gel** over the window and leave the tungsten-balanced light unfiltered. In that case the daylight passing through the orange gel is converted to match the tungsten-balanced light source in the room and no filtration will be needed on a film camera when shooting tungsten-balanced film. Daylight-balanced film would require a blue (80A) filter to convert the tungsten-balanced light to the color balance of the film. A video camera would be set to its tungsten preset or manually white balanced.

Of course, there are times when mixed light sources can be acceptable and can even be quite beautiful. In a shot in which a character is sitting near a campfire, one side of the character's face might be lit by an orange light motivated by the firelight. The other side of his face might be illuminated by a blue fill light, creating the impression of moonlight. There are, of course, different degrees of orange and blue, and it is a matter of taste as to how subtle or pronounced the difference between the two sides of the character's face should be.

Sometimes beginning filmmakers are confused by the use of the terms "hot," "warm" and "cool" in discussions of lighting, color and exposure. In a lighting set-up a light that is too bright might be referred to as being too "hot." In the same way an overexposed shot might be called "hot." When discussing color it is common to call colors at the blue end of the spectrum "cool" and to refer to those at the red end of the spectrum as "warm." These are common slang uses of these terms. Such usage can be confusing, because in scientific discussions of color temperature blue light has a higher **color temperature** than red light.

Color temperature, while related in theory to actual physical temperatures, does not indicate the amount of heat generated by a light source, nor does it measure the burning temperature of a lamp's filament. Instead, the color temperature of a light source indicates the color quality of the source. It indicates whether the light source is biased toward the red or blue part of the spectrum or somewhere in between.

Color temperature is measured in **Kelvins** (K). The two important color temperatures to remember are the color temperature of tungsten-balanced movie lights (3200 K) and that of daylight (5500 K). A color temperature of 3200 Kelvin indicates a light source that is orange in its color quality. 5500 K indicates a bluish light. Different kinds of light sources produce various colors of light, even though most people don't usually notice the differences. The human brain has the ability to adapt to situations that are not too extreme, making the light from most sources appear as neutral white light without a strong bias. But film stocks cannot adapt in that way. A color film stock must be manufactured to reproduce color correctly under one specific type of light. 3200 K was established as the standard color temperature for tungsten light, and all professional tungsten-balanced color film stocks are manufactured to reproduce color properly when exposed under light of that color temperature. Tungsten-balanced color film will reproduce colors correctly when it is used in combination with tungsten-balanced movie lights. Some color films are daylight balanced. They are manufactured to be exposed under light with a color temperature of 5500 K. Video is more flexible than film in its ability to be white balanced to the light in the scene. This does not, however, eliminate the need to use gels in order to make mixed color sources match each other. When setting white balance, video cameras use a daylight preset of 5600 K, which is not visibly different from 5500 K.

What happens when film stock is exposed under light of the wrong color temperature? Tungsten-balanced film exposed in the relatively blue light of daylight will look blue unless an orange 85 filter is used to correct the daylight, converting its color temperature from 5500 K to the color temperature for which the film is balanced, 3200 K. Orange 85 filters are built into the optical system of all super-8 cameras. Built-in filters are rarely found in 16mm cameras, so it is necessary to put a glass filter on the front of the lens. If the camera has a filter slot behind the lens, a gelatin filter can be used in the slot. The 85 filter is put in place when shooting tungsten-balanced color film in daylight, and it is removed when shooting under movie lights. Daylight-balanced color film would look orange if exposed under tungsten-balanced lights without any color-correcting filtration. A blue 80A filter is used to convert 3200 K light to 5500 K, the daylight color temperature (see Chapter 2, *Film Camera and Film Stock*). Black-and-white films are not affected by color temperature in any significant way, and they can always be exposed in either daylight or tungsten light without any filtration. As long as the light in a shot is consistent in its color quality, a video camera can simply be manually white balanced in order to make colors reproduce properly in that shot.

Light Intensity

The **intensity** of light on a subject is dependent upon two things; the brightness of the light source and its distance from the subject. Light intensity can be measured in units known as **footcandles**. One footcandle is defined as the amount of light a so-called "standard candle" would cast upon a subject from one foot away. Footcandles are the most widely accepted standard unit of light measurement when measuring the light falling on a subject. The intensity of light on a subject decreases as the subject moves farther from the light source. This **fall-off** in intensity is more pronounced when the subject is close to the light source. If an actor is three feet from the light and moves another foot away, the intensity of the light on the actor will be noticeably diminished at the new distance. If the actor is thirty feet away and moves back another foot, there will be no perceptible change in light intensity.

When shooting film, light intensity is measured with a handheld incident light meter or a reflected meter and an 18% gray card. In most situations filmmakers prefer incident light meters. An incident light meter is like a reflected light meter with a built-in gray card. While incident meters are a little more convenient to use, a reflected light meter used properly with an 18% gray card is equivalent to using an incident light meter (see Chapter 4, *The Lens*). When shooting video, intensity is usually judged by using a properly calibrated monitor or viewfinder.

Three-Point Lighting

Very few scenes are lit by a single light source. Usually, several lighting units are involved. A common approach to lighting a subject combines three lights, each one serving a specific purpose. Three-point lighting frequently makes use of both hard and soft light sources and always involves a variety of lighting angles and intensities. The **key light** is the primary source of illumination and may be a hard or soft light source depending upon the mood of the scene. It is often placed roughly 45 degrees off the camera/subject axis

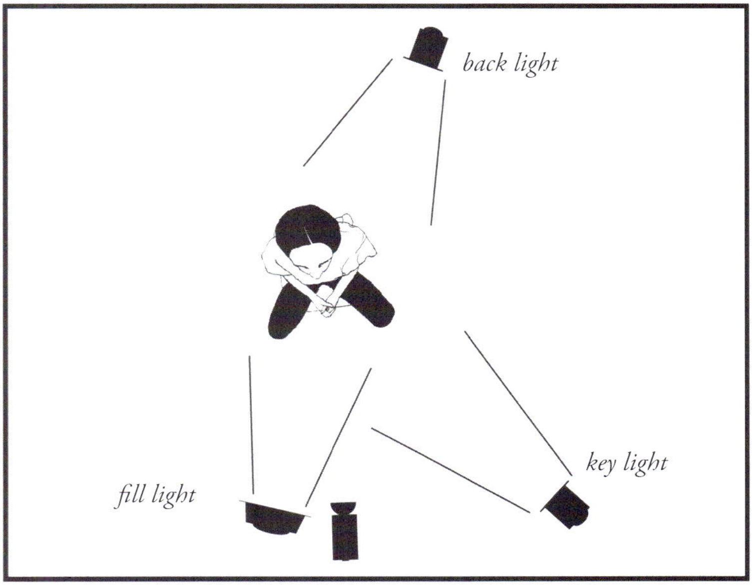

A three-point lighting diagram.

and above the subject. This light produces modeling (or a shadow pattern) that helps give the subject a three-dimensional appearance. Since the shadows created by the key light are usually too dark on film or video, a second light, the **fill light**, is used to illuminate the shadow areas to some degree. The fill light is not as intense as the key light, so the key light shadows are not completely filled in. The fill light is almost always a soft light source so that it doesn't create a distinct second set of shadows. It is normally placed close to the camera/subject axis at eye level or higher. From this position any shadows created by the fill light will be hidden behind the subject from the camera's vantage point.

The third light is the **back light**, placed behind the subject and high enough to be out of the frame. This is often a hard light and it is positioned to create an outline of light around the subject's head and shoulders. Without this outline the subject tends to blend into the background. The back light separates the subject from the background, adding apparent depth to the shot. The subject looks like a three-dimensional person in front of a wall rather than a flat image on the wall.

In many cases a fourth light source, a **background light**, is used. This light is positioned to illuminate the background but not the subject. Like a back light, it is useful in creating separation and depth between the subject and the background, and it can also help by minimizing unwanted shadows on the background. Sometimes a three-light set-up consists of a key light, a fill light and a background light rather than a back light. The background light separates the subject from the background without the often unmotivated outline of light that a back light creates.

When lighting a shot with two or more actors, a three-point lighting set-up is not always needed for each actor. Sometimes one fill light can cover the whole shot, with perhaps an individual key light for each character. If two characters are facing each other, **cross-lighting** might be more economical. In cross-lighting two lights are used to create a crossing pattern of light, so that each light acts as one character's back light and the other character's key light at the same time. A single fill light positioned near the camera can fill in the shadows. (See p. 152 for a cross-lighting diagram.)

Key light only.

Key light plus fill light.

Key light plus fill light with back light and background light.

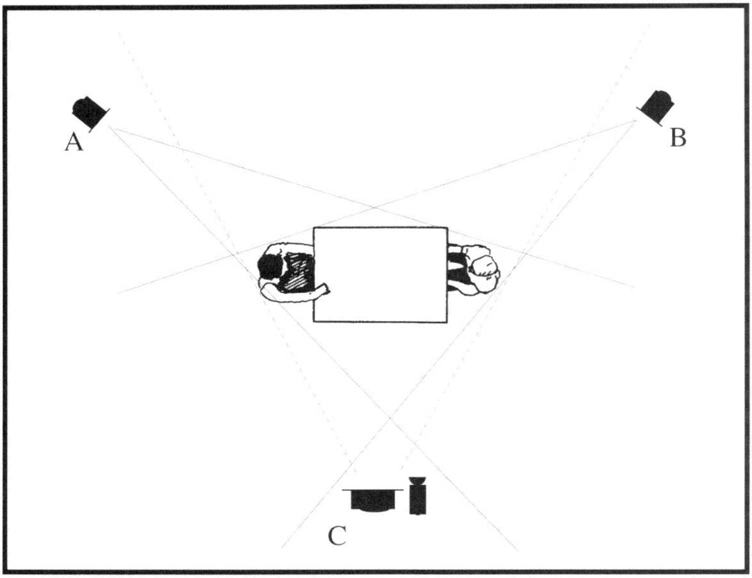

A cross-lighting diagram. Lights A and B each serve as a key light for one character and as a back light for the other, while light C is a fill light for both.

Lighting Contrast

In any lighting set-up it is important to control the **lighting contrast ratio**. This is a measure of the difference in light intensity between the brighter and darker sides of a subject. These areas can be referred to as the **highlight** and **shadow** areas. Since the highlight area will usually be lit by both the key light and the fill light, and the shadow will only be lit by the fill light, the lighting contrast ratio can be expressed as the ratio *key + fill : fill*. Using the light on an actor's face as an example, if the highlight side of the face (the key light plus the fill light) is twice as bright as the shadow side of the face (the fill light alone), then the lighting contrast ratio is 2:1.

Different lighting contrast ratios suggest different moods on film. Traditionally, higher ratios are used for more dramatic scenes, while low ratios are typically used for less serious moments. Knowing the lighting contrast ratio in a scene helps a filmmaker to visualize how the light will look on film, which is usually very different from the way it appears to the eye.

2:1 lighting contrast ratio.

4:1 lighting contrast ratio.

8:1 lighting contrast ratio.

16:1 lighting contrast ratio.

The same subject shot with different lighting contrast ratios.

While filmmakers shooting film learn how different lighting contrast ratios will translate to various film stocks, those shooting on video pay attention to contrast ratios too. Knowing that video has more limited latitude than negative film, it is usual to establish lighting ratios that are lower than they might be if shooting on film. Measuring ratios when shooting video is also useful in order to maintain lighting consistency throughout a scene that might consist of many shots that are shot out of sequence. Of course, a properly calibrated monitor or viewfinder is the main tool for determining what looks right.

Lighting contrast ratios can be easily measured using an incident light meter. First, take a reading by holding the meter in front of the subject so that it is hit by both the key light and the fill light (the highlight). Take a second reading holding the meter so that it is hit by the fill light alone (the shadow area). You can take the second reading by either shading the meter from the key light or by turning the key light off while reading the light. If the highlight area of the subject is illuminated by 200 footcandles and the shadow area by 100 footcandles of light, the ratio is 2:1. If the highlight reads 1,000 footcandles and the shadow 100 footcandles, the ratio is 10:1. While it requires a little more effort to measure a contrast ratio using a reflected light meter, it can be done effectively by taking two reflected light readings from an 18% gray card. First, hold the gray card in front of the actor's face so that the light from both the key light and the fill light hits the card and fully illuminates it. Suppose the light meter reads f/4 in this case. Take a second reading with the gray card positioned so that only the fill light falls on it. To do this shade the card so that your body blocks the key light, or simply turn the key light off. Suppose the light meter reads f/2.8 now. The bright side of the face is one stop brighter than the darker side. A one f-stop difference in the two light readings means that the highlight is twice as bright as the shadow (see "Exposure" in Chapter 4, *The Lens*), so the lighting contrast ratio is 2:1. Moving the key light closer to the subject or using a brighter light might result in readings of f/5.6 in the highlight area and f/2.8 in the shadow area. (Notice that the intensity of the fill light doesn't change even though the key light is brighter.) Now the difference is two stops, a 4:1 ratio. (As the lens is opened from f/5.6 to f/4 to f/2.8, the size of the lens iris is doubled and doubled again.) A three stop difference indicates an 8:1 ratio; a four stop difference indicates a 16:1 ratio and so on.

You can use this method of measuring lighting contrast ratios in other situations. If you are shooting outside and have one actor standing in the sun and another in the shade, you would take one light reading in the sunny area and another in the shaded area. Often the resulting ratio will be unacceptably high, and you won't be able to do anything to reduce it. If you can't reposition the actors or add light to the shaded area, you will have to decide which is more important in the scene, the highlight area or the shadow area, and choose an f-stop accordingly. Usually, you will want to expose the film properly for the most important part of the composition. Sometimes, in high contrast situations, it is useful to shift the exposure slightly in order to preserve some detail in other areas of the frame.

Contrast ratios are especially important when working with reversal film because of its limited latitude (see Chapter 2, *The Film Camera and Film Stock*). Reversal film has a very limited tolerance for overexposure and underexposure. If the shadow areas in the frame are underexposed by more than three stops they will start to lose detail, and the shadows will be rendered as undifferentiated black. If the highlights are overexposed by more than one stop they will begin to burn out. If the contrast ratio is higher than 16:1 (a four stop difference) no matter which intermediate f-stop you choose for exposing the film, you cannot avoid either overexposing the highlights or underexposing the shadows to the point that substantial detail is lost. In this case it is necessary to add fill light to bring the lighting contrast ratio down to an acceptable level. Negative film has a much wider latitude. Shadow areas can be underexposed by three or more stops without losing detail, while highlights can be overexposed by three or four stops without completely burning out.

Motivated Light

When planning any lighting set-up a primary consideration is whether the light is **motivated** or **unmotivated**. Motivated light is rationalized by a source that is either shown or suggested within the scene. If a character is sitting next to a bright window and the side of her face that is closer to the window is brighter than the side that is farther from the window, then the bright light on her face is explained or motivated by the presence of the window, even if the light hitting the actor's face is actually coming from a source used to imitate the window light. In another example, if a room is bathed in red light but no red light source has been established in the room, then this red light is unmotivated. If another shot has established that there is a red neon sign outside the window, then the red light inside the room is motivated. A good example of motivated lighting appears in Atom Egoyan's 1995 film, *Exotica*. As two characters sit in a parked car during a heavy rain, a moving pattern of dappled light illuminates their faces. This effect is motivated by the streetlights shining through the rain-covered windshield. In this example the lighting accentuates the sad, disturbed state of one of the characters, but it does this subtly because it is motivated by the physical setting.

Night Shooting

When shooting a night scene there is almost never enough available light to create a pleasing image. Street lights or moonlight, even though they create enough light for human vision, have practically no effect on most film stocks. Many video cameras can shoot in low light conditions, but often this is accomplished by increasing the gain and shooting with the iris wide open, both of which have a negative effect on image quality.

The most convincing way to shoot an outdoor night scene is to shoot **night-for-night**. This means shooting in the dark and using lighting units to selectively illuminate and highlight the scene. It isn't necessary or even desirable to fully illuminate everything since the idea is to make it look like night, but night-for-night shooting can still be difficult. If the shot is a long shot or an extreme long shot, it might require many powerful lighting units to light it. In most productions that translates to a great deal of time and expense. So, in some cases filmmakers choose to shoot **day-for-night**.

Day-for-night shooting involves shooting a night scene on a bright sunny day. Usually, this is done by underexposing and shooting late in the afternoon or early in the morning when the sun is low in the sky and shadows are long. It is also necessary to avoid showing any sky in the shots, as it is too bright and destroys the illusion. Some filmmakers put a blue filter over the lens to make the image look a little bluish, since it is an old filmmaking convention that moonlight is blue. Day-for-night shots are usually underexposed by one or two stops. The position of the sun in relation to the subject is important. The sunlight should hit the subject from the side or even from behind. The sunlight outlines the subject but much of it is left in the dark, underexposed shadows. Day-for-night shots won't work if the day is overcast. They require hard sunlight. Unfortunately, even at their best day-for-night scenes frequently look very artificial.

Another alternative is to shoot **dusk-for-night**. Dusk-for-night involves shooting in that very short period of time after the sun goes down, when street lights and business signs and car headlights are on, but while the sky is still bright and there is enough light to expose the film. Again, all shots must avoid showing the bright sky. The first few shots might be intentionally underexposed, but very soon there will be barely enough light for shooting, and then not enough. Since there will be about half an hour of usable light in the summer and even less in the winter, shooting must be done quickly and efficiently. Since they require fast shooting, dusk-for-night sequences have to be well planned ahead of time.

Lighting Tools

Lights can have a number of features. Every light has a **socket** in which the lamp can be mounted. A bare light bulb at the end of an extension cord might illuminate (or at least seem to illuminate) a scene in a mechanic's garage. That is as basic a lighting unit as there is, but almost all movie lights have a **reflector** in addition to the socket. The scoop-shaped reflector directs the beam of light. The shape of the reflector and its position in relation to the lamp are the main factors that determine the quality of light the source emits. Most lighting units also include **barndoors** which are useful in shaping the beam of light. Barndoors are hinged metal flaps that mount in front of the reflector, and they can be partially opened or closed to achieve the appropriate effect. They can be helpful in shielding one area of a shot from light that is intended to illuminate another part of the frame. Some lights include a focusing mechanism, a knob or lever that can move either the reflector or the lamp forward and backward, altering the quality of light as the

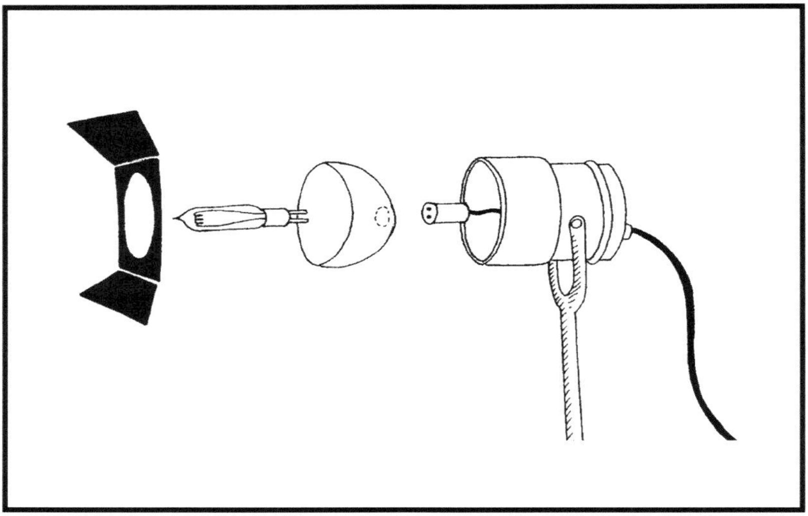

A basic diagram of a light showing the barndoors, lamp, reflector, socket and housing.

physical relationship between the reflector and the lamp changes. When the reflector and lamp are close together, they create rays of light that are more nearly parallel, resulting in a hard, narrow "spotlight." When the reflector and lamp are farther apart, the light has more opportunity to bounce from a wider variety of points inside the reflector. The rays of light that are emitted are less parallel, and a slightly softer and broader "floodlight" results.

Two types of basic lighting instruments are used for many location lighting situations. Standard **incandescent lamps** are designed like the old style of conventional household light bulbs. They are easy to handle, comparatively inexpensive and can be found in sizes ranging up to 500 watts. At higher wattage these standard incandescent lamps become very large and cumbersome. **Quartz-halogen lamps** are more efficient than standard incandescents in that they create much more light intensity for their size. They are more difficult to handle and more expensive, but because of their size they allow much greater mobility during shooting.

A standard incandescent light consists of a tungsten **filament** that glows when it is heated, and the filament is surrounded by a standard glass bulb or **envelope**. As the filament burns, the tungsten evaporates and creates black deposits on the inside of the glass envelope. Because of this trait standard incandescent lamps lose intensity and change color slightly as they age.

Quartz-halogen (or simply "quartz") lamps also have a tungsten filament. Their envelope is made of quartz glass, a softer, more porous and much more delicate type of glass. Quartz lamps burn at higher physical temperatures than standard incandescent lamps do, and their porous glass envelope allows heat to escape. The quartz envelope is filled with halogen gas. When the tungsten filament evaporates during use, evaporated tungsten combines with halogen gas and is re-deposited onto the filament, not on the inside of the glass envelope. While this does not stop the lamp from burning out with age, it does allow a quartz-halogen lamp to maintain constant intensity and color throughout its life. The quartz glass envelope of a quartz-halogen lamp is extremely delicate. It should never be touched since the oil from your fingers will weaken the glass, causing the lamp to burn out prematurely or even bubble and explode. Since quartz lamps are very expensive, and exploding hot glass is hazardous, be careful to handle quartz lamps properly.

Chapter 11

Sound

The earliest movies were considered "silent" films, but many of them included some kind of aural accompaniment, or **soundtrack**, to enhance the visual content of the film. At first musicians performed this accompaniment. Later, technical advances made it possible to mechanically record sound to be played back in synchronization with the images on the film (**sync sound**). Conversely, the earliest television shows were essentially "radio with pictures" that depended on sound more than visuals for their effect. Regardless of whether a film is shot in 16mm, super-8 film or in a video format, digital post-production offers quite a bit of control and many creative options in the creation of a soundtrack. A well-made soundtrack can enhance a film, but poorly recorded audio or a sloppily designed soundtrack can ruin even the most visually beautiful film.

Characteristics of Sound

Sound can be thought of as a disturbance in the air, like the disturbance created in water when a rock is thrown into a pond. When an object like a guitar string vibrates, waves of air pressure move through the air like ripples traveling through water. As the string moves in one direction it pushes the air in that direction, causing a wave of increased air pressure. When the string pulls back it creates a trough of lower air pressure. As this action is repeated many times each second, a series of pressure waves are formed which move through the air. When they reach the ear they cause the eardrum to vibrate back and forth with the changes in air pressure. A series of bones and nerves are connected to the eardrum, and they convert this pattern of air pressure changes into a pattern of electrical impulses that travel to the brain. The brain translates these electrical impulses into our sensory perception of sound.

The Sine Wave

The waves of air pressure created when a simple sound is generated can be diagrammed into a regularly repeating pattern called a sine wave. This diagram can be used to describe the characteristics of the sound itself. The height of the wave indicates the sound's volume or **amplitude**. The greater the amplitude the louder the sound seems to be. Amplitude is measured in **decibels** (**dB**). The decibel scale is geometric rather than linear. An increase of 10dB means a doubling of the amplitude; a 10dB sound is twice as loud as a 0dB sound and a 30dB sound is four times as loud as a 10dB sound. 0dB is considered the "threshold of hearing." Any sound softer than 0dB does not deflect the eardrum enough to register as a sound. Approximately 130dB is considered the "threshold of pain." Sounds louder than 130dB begin to overload the auditory system and can damage the ear. The **dynamic range** of a sound receiving device is the range from the softest sound it can register to the loudest sound it can handle. Therefore, the dynamic range of the human ear is about 130dB. The dynamic range of a sound producer is the range from the softest to the loudest sound produced. The dynamic range of a summer storm might vary from the rustle of the wind in the trees to a loud clap of thunder directly overhead.

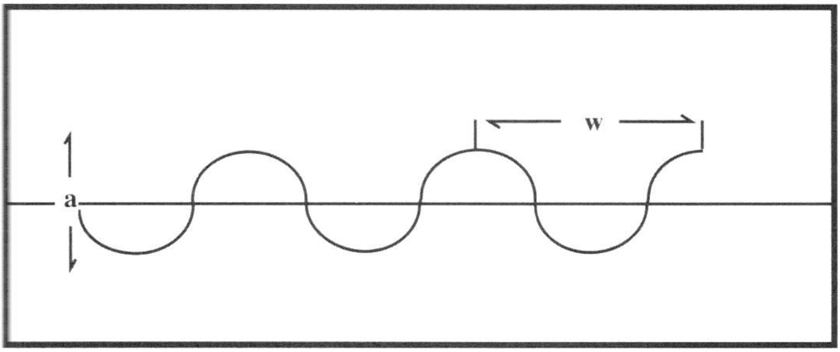

A sine wave diagram showing amplitude (a) and wavelength (w).

Measuring the distance one cycle of a sine wave covers, from crest to crest or trough to trough, is a measure of the **wavelength**. Large objects, like a cello string, vibrate slowly and produce sound with a long wavelength. Small objects, like a violin string, vibrate more quickly, resulting in sound with a shorter wavelength. A longer wavelength means that fewer cycles of the sine wave will occur in a given length of time. The longer the wavelength, the fewer sound wave cycles strike the ear in a given amount of time. Therefore, a sound with a longer wavelength is said to have a lower **frequency**. Frequency is measured in "cycles per second," or **Hertz** (**Hz**). Lower frequency sounds are often called **bass**, while higher frequency sounds are known as **treble**. Any sound with a frequency lower than approximately 20Hz is felt as an actual vibration rather than being heard as a sound. A sound with a frequency higher than 20,000Hz does not register on the human eardrum enough to register as a sound, but animals such as dogs and bats can hear sounds at these high frequencies. The approximate **frequency range** of the human ear is from 20Hz to 20,000Hz.

Microphones

Sound can be collected, recorded, stored and reproduced by an electronic audio system that mimics human hearing in certain ways. A **microphone** is the part of an audio system that captures sound. The microphone contains a wafer-thin diaphragm that vibrates back and forth like the human eardrum does when sound waves hit it. In a **dynamic microphone** a metal pin is attached to the diaphragm and a coil of wire is attached to the metal pin. The vibration of the diaphragm causes the coil of wire to move back and forth within a magnetic field. This movement causes changes in the voltage signal that travels from the microphone through a cable to a recording device.

In a dynamic microphone these voltage signals are very weak. Soft sounds that deflect the diaphragm only slightly may create a signal so weak that it cannot be transmitted from the microphone. Dynamic microphones are frequently described as being self

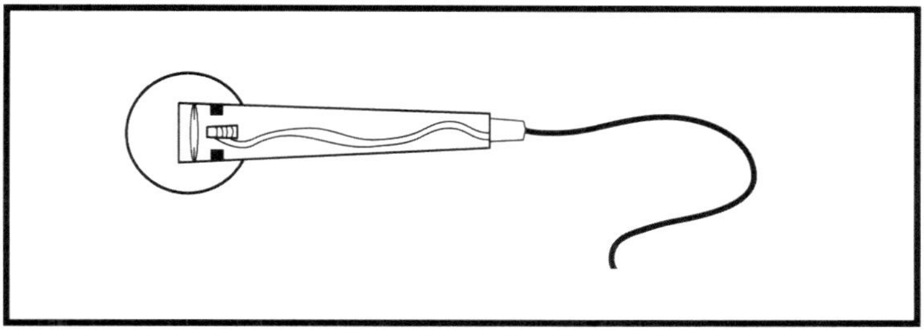

A simple microphone.

powered, relying only on the actual air pressure of the sound to create a signal. A **condenser microphone** uses a power source, either a battery inside the microphone or a separate power supply, to amplify the voltage signal, allowing even soft sounds to be recorded. Condenser microphones are best suited to situations in which the sound is soft. They are also useful when the sound is coming from far away, since sound dissipates with distance. For this reason condenser mics are commonly used during sync sound shooting, since the microphone must usually be placed some distance from the action in order to keep it out of the frame.

Pick-up Patterns

Even though sound dissipates, becoming softer as it travels through the air, distance is not the only factor that determines how well a sound is picked up by a microphone. If it were, then a person speaking ten feet in front of a microphone would register just as clearly as a person speaking ten feet behind it, beside it or anywhere on the perimeter of a circle ten feet from the microphone. Certain microphones do work in this way; they are referred to as **omnidirectional** microphones. They receive sound equally well from all directions and a diagram of the microphone's **pick-up pattern** is depicted as a circle, either drawn on the microphone itself or in an accompanying manual.

In most film and video work an omnidirectional pick-up pattern is not useful. While a sound recordist typically wants to clearly record the voice of an actor in front of the microphone, there are usually sounds coming from behind the microphone such as the sound of the camera running, which are undesirable and should not be recorded. In such a situation the recordist would choose a *directional* microphone that does not register sounds coming from behind the mic as distinctly as those sounds coming from the front or the sides of the microphone. Because the pick-up pattern of this type of microphone is heart shaped, it is called a **cardioid** microphone. A microphone with a narrower pick-up pattern that does not register sounds coming from the sides as clearly as those sounds coming from the front is called **hypercardioid** or **supercardioid**. These microphones, with their extremely narrow pick-up patterns, are commonly referred to as **shotgun** microphones. When recording an actor with a shotgun microphone it is important to aim the microphone directly at the actor's mouth. Because of its narrow pick-up pattern, if the microphone is positioned *off-axis*, the actor's voice will sound muffled in the recording.

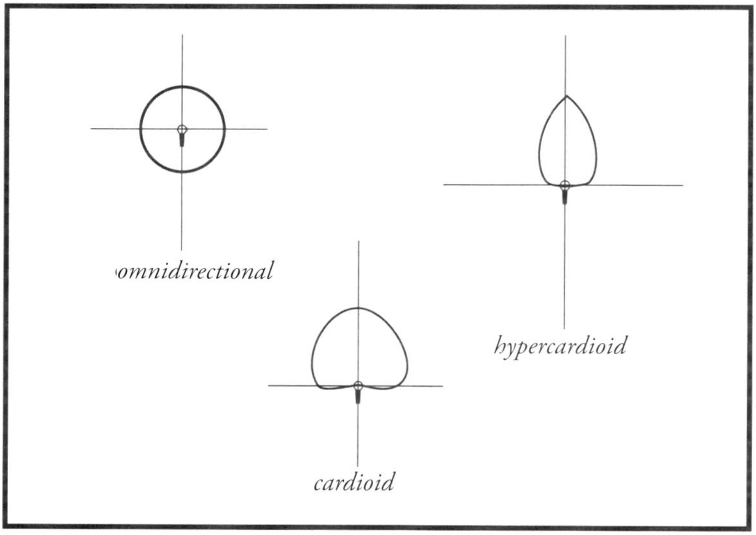

Pick-up patterns of an omnidirectional, cardioid and hypercardioid microphone.

While microphones are sometimes handheld, they are usually mounted on a **boom**, a long pole that allows the microphone to be held outside the frame and maneuvered above an actor. However, in some situations a **lavaliere** microphone is used. Lavalieres are extremely small. In some cases lavaliere microphones are no larger than a pencil eraser. They are almost always condenser microphones, and they frequently have an omnidirectional pick-up pattern. The lavaliere microphone is fastened to an actor's clothes, usually the shirt, and the mic and cable are hidden beneath the clothing. A lavaliere microphone is useful when even a long boom cannot get a microphone close enough to the actor to record dialogue clearly. A *wireless* lavaliere mic allows an actor to be photographed in long shots while his dialogue is recorded. A lavaliere microphone can also be hidden on a set more easily than a larger microphone.

It is important to remember that even though a microphone works like the human ear does in some ways, it does not have the ability to selectively hear or concentrate on certain sounds while excluding others. A microphone's selectivity is limited to the directional qualities of its pick-up pattern, but sounds outside a microphone's pick-up pattern are not completely inaudible; they are simply received and transmitted with less clarity and at a lower level.

When recording sound such as dialogue that must be heard clearly on the soundtrack, the key is to get the microphone as close to the subject as possible. This allows the dialogue to be recorded very clearly without picking up unwanted sounds that may be present in the recording environment. When the mic is closer to the person who is speaking, the recording level can be turned down, and softer environmental noises will be recorded at a proportionally lower level. The use of a boom to hold the microphone just above the top of the frame (and within a few inches of the actor's head) or a lavaliere to keep the microphone on the actor's person, are both strategies meant to help in recording clear, "clean" dialogue.

For this reason it is almost never a good idea to use a microphone mounted on the camera, such as the onboard microphone on a video camera. To get a good shot the camera almost always has to be positioned too far away from the subject to get clean sound. A camera-mounted microphone is perfectly positioned, however, to pick up the unwanted sounds of the camera operator and the camera itself.

Recording sound using a microphone on a boom.

Analog Audio Recording

Analog audio recording is very similar to recording video on analog videotape (See Chapter 3, *The Video Camera and Recorder*) though it is somewhat simpler. In analog audio systems, the voltage signal created in the microphone travels to a **tape recorder** that encodes a corresponding pattern of electromagnetic changes onto audiotape coated with magnetically sensitive particles of iron oxide. Audiotape can be packaged in cassettes that load into a cassette recorder like a videotape loads into a camcorder. Tape is also sold on reels that must be manually threaded through a "reel-to-reel" tape recorder.

When the electronic signals from a microphone reach the record head of a recorder, they cause voltage fluctuations in the field of a magnetic coil in the head. As the tape passes over the record head this changing magnetic field creates a specific pattern of magnetism in the tape's oxide particles. When the tape passes over a playback head, the head reads the magnetic pattern of the oxide particles and converts it into a series of varying voltages that can be amplified and sent to a speaker. The voltage signals cause paper cones to vibrate in the speaker, and the vibration of the cones reproduces the range of frequencies and amplitudes of the original sound with more or less accuracy, depending upon the quality of the audio system. In analog recorders, the amplitude and frequency information of the voltage signal is a direct translation of the amplitude and frequency information of the sound. Changing the voltage signal changes the sound quality. This can be an intentional change, such as increasing the amplitude of the voltage to make the sound louder, or it can be unintentional. For instance, imperfections in the tape or variations in tape speed can affect the voltage signal and cause distortions in the sound.

It is simpler to lay down a magnetic pattern on a blank tape than it is to use a tape with a previous pattern encoded on it, since the old magnetic pattern must be changed at the same time that the new one is recorded. For this reason, in addition to their record and playback heads, tape recorders use an erase head that produces a constant magnetic field to destroy any previously recorded signal just before new information is recorded.

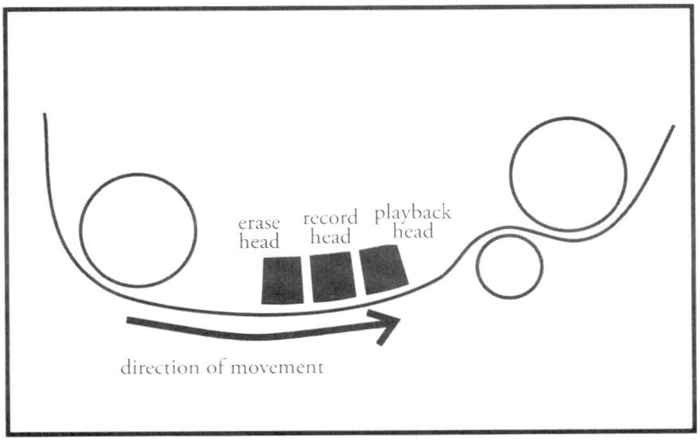

A three-headed recorder showing erase, record and playback heads. Some recorders contain a combined record/playback head, making them two-headed rather than three-headed machines.

Digital Audio Recording

Just as analog audio recording is similar to analog video recording, digital audio recording is much like digital video recording. Audio usually contains much less information than video, making the process simpler.

Since microphones produce analog signals, these signals must be converted into digital signals in order to make digital recordings. This is done in a part of the digital audio recorder called an analog-to-digital converter (A-D converter). High quality A-D converters typically have high bit rates so that the sound can be recreated with very little degradation. Amplifiers and loudspeakers are also analog devices. Playing back from a digital audio device into an amplifier requires a conversion of the digital audio into an analog signal. This is done in the digital recorder's digital-to-analog converter (D-A converter).

Once a digital recording has been made, it can be copied many times without loss of quality as long as it is not converted from digital to analog. Converting a digital audio signal into analog form and then recording it with another digital device will result in a loss of quality. Quality will also be lost if the audio signal remains in digital form but the sample rate or the bit rate are changed.

When a recording is made on a digital recorder, the A-D converter samples the incoming audio signal from the microphone and converts it into binary numbers. The sampling rate indicates how many times per second the sound is sampled and it is measured in kilohertz (kHz), or thousands of cycles per second. Higher sampling rates produce better quality sound since more samples result in more pieces of information, more accurately reproducing the sound wave. The bit rate is the size of the range of possible number values used to record each sample. Higher bit rates result in a larger range of possible values, and a larger range of possible values means a more precise representation of the sound wave. 8-bit sound has only 256 possible values. 16-bit sound has 65,536 possible values and will create a much more detailed representation of the sound wave. A variety of sample rates and bit rates are in use at this time. When using audio from a variety of sources (video camcorder, CD, audio recorder, etc) it is a good idea to make sure that all of the sampling rates and bit rates match. Otherwise, when the audio from disparate sources is edited together it may be necessary to render much of the audio and could result in subtle distortions in the sound.

One digital audio format currently used by many professional film sound recordists is **Digital Audio Tape** (**DAT**). DAT recorders typically use a sample rate of 48kHz or 44.1kHz and a bit rate of 16 or 24 bits. Many DAT recorders can record SMPTE time code along with the audio signal. This allows them to run in precise synchronization with video recorders and with other devices that use SMPTE time code. Audio with SMPTE time code can also be easily synchronized with film that has been transferred to video.

Most digital recorders record to solid-state storage such as **Compact Flash** cards. Compact Flash cards and other similar memory cards are reusable and available in a wide range of storage capacities. Often digital recorders using solid-state storage can create files in a variety of sampling rates, bit rates and file types. Some of these devices use SMPTE timecode, but many do not, and the audio must be manually synchronized with the picture during post-production.

Single-System Sound

During **single-system sound** shooting, sound and image are recorded on the same strip of material in the same machine at the same time. Although single-system sound was once used in both the 16mm and super-8 formats, using a strip of magnetic oxide coated onto one edge of the film, it has been obsolete in film for some time.

Film moves through a camera gate in an intermittent movement (see Chapter 2: *The Film Camera and Film Stock*), but intermittent movement across an audio record head would result in badly distorted sound. Because of this the record head in a single-system film camera could not be positioned in or near the camera gate. It had to be located in a part of the camera in which the film traveled at a constant rate. Consequently, the image was captured at a different place on the strand of film than its corresponding sound. There was a gap between sound and image. Problems arose when making a physical edit, since both the image and the sound were cut in the same place, even though the image and sound on any given frame did not correspond to each other.

On the other hand most video shooting is done single-system. Since video does not feature intermittent movement, recording audio onto the same tape or within the same digital file is not a problem, and it helps to avoid synchronization problems in post-production. It also makes the crew smaller and reduces equipment needs. The drawback of single-system shooting is that the same operator is usually responsible for both video and audio during shooting. When things get hectic or rushed it is almost always sound quality that gets sacrificed, causing problems that often can only be solved through reshooting. Remember that recording high-quality single-system sound on video requires the use of an external microphone attached to the camera by a cable or a wireless transmitter, not the on-camera microphone.

Double-System Sound

All sync-sound films and many videos are shot using **double-system sound**. The sound and image are recorded simultaneously, but on separate machines: the sound is recorded in a recorder that is separate from the camera, while the image is photographed onto the film or recorded onto a digital video format. In double-system shooting the camera and audio recorder must run in synchronization. If they drift out of synchronization by even one frame the viewer will notice that the sound does not properly match the image.

When shooting film synchronization can be achieved by linking the camera and an analog recorder with a cable. Although it is used infrequently today, **cable sync** features a properly outfitted film camera generating a pulse that travels through the cable to a **sync head** in the recorder. The **sync pulse** is laid down on the tape on a channel that is separate from the audio channel. Because the number of sync pulses laid down on the tape are in direct proportion to the number of frames that move through the camera, the sync pulse becomes an effective reference for putting picture and sound in sync. This reference is crucial if the sound on the magnetic tape will be re-recorded (or transferred) onto **magnetic fullcoat**. Fullcoat is essentially thick sprocketed magnetic tape with dimensions that match those of the film format (16mm or 35mm). During the sound transfer the sync pulse on the sync channel is used as a reference to precisely control the playback speed of the tape, ensuring that for every frame of picture there will be one corresponding frame of audio on magnetic full-coat. Since the width and sprocketing of the fullcoat are identical to those of the film, the two strands can be easily synchronized during editing. Shooting cable sync places limitations on the mobility of both the camera and the tape recorder, because they are physically linked by the sync cable. Also, cable-sync is only viable with analog workflows using audio tape and fullcoat, which have almost completely disappeared at this point.

Crystal sync uses quartz crystal technology rather than a cable to ensure synchronization. The camera and recorder are not physically joined. A crystal in the film camera precisely controls the speed of the camera motor and, therefore, its per-second frame rate. It ensures that the camera runs at exactly 24 fps. A separate crystal in the analog audio recorder generates an equally precise sync pulse. The crystal in the recorder does not control the running speed of the machine, but it does generate a pre-determined number of sync pulses that are exact in relation to time (60 pulses for every second of real time). Because the crystal in the camera and the crystal in the recorder both function with the utmost accuracy in relation to real time, during the transfer to magnetic fullcoat the sync pulses on the tape will serve as a reference, ensuring a frame-to-frame correspondence between picture and sound. The audio corresponding to 60 pulses on the tape will be transferred onto 24 frames on magnetic fullcoat. When double-system material is edited, the picture and the magnetic fullcoat can be cut separately but in exact relation to each other. As an alternative to the conventional analog workflow, a filmmaker could opt to shoot crystal sync material and then transfer the audio from the analog magnetic tape to a digital file (using an A-D converter) for editing. In this case, of course, the film negative would also be transferred to a digital format.

While crystal sync and cable sync systems were developed for film cameras in conjunction with analog audio recorders, the vast majority of films today follow digital workflows. The sampling rate of a digital audio recorder is extremely precise. If shooting digital video the sampling rate of the video recorder is equally precise. Two digital machines running simultaneously will remain in sync over extremely long takes and can be combined in a digital editing system with no synchronization problems. A crystal-sync film camera will also remain in sync with a digital audio recorder for at least 15 minutes. Since filmmakers typically use camera magazines that hold 11 minutes of film or less (and since individual takes on film that exceed that length are almost unheard of), the film can be synchronized with the audio with no problems.

When editing double-system sound there must be some sync point that allows the editor to match the picture with the sound. Most filmmakers working in double-system use a **slate**, a black or white board with sticks that can be clapped. During shooting a crew member claps the sticks together in front of the camera, with both camera and audio recorder running, at the beginning of every take. This makes it very easy to match the exact frame (on the picture track) where the sticks meet with the exact moment (on the audio track) where the sound of the clap begins. Once those two frames are lined up on a flatbed film editor or in a digital timeline, the shot should be in sync and should remain that way for the remainder of the take. If both camera and recorder have SMPTE timecode, then picture and sound can be placed in sync more quickly by matching timecode numbers.

Sound Editing and Mixing

Most films combine sync-sound dialogue with **post-dubbed** music and sound effects. Post-dubbed sound is recorded after shooting has been completed, during the editing process. While precise synchronization such as that required when trying to post-dub extensive dialogue is problematic, some films are entirely post-dubbed due to budgetary and aesthetic considerations. Post-dubbed films usually utilize some combination of dialogue, music, sound effects (such as footsteps or a telephone ringing) and **voice-over** narration in which one of the film's characters or a narrator speaks on the soundtrack but does not appear on the screen.

More often, sync-sound dialogue is recorded on the set using single-system or double-system sound. This dialogue is synchronized and edited with the picture and combined with music and sound effects. The music can be composed specifically for the film, or the filmmaker can obtain the rights to pre-existing songs and musical compositions. Sound effects may be recorded on the set during shooting if they cannot be reproduced later, but they are always recorded separately from dialogue. Most often, the optimum microphone position and level for recording clear dialogue are not best for recording sound effects. In addition, the actual sound, even if recorded well, may not be satisfactory. The sound of knuckles hitting a jaw is not very dramatic or powerful, so action films often create the sound of a "punch" that sounds more like a side of beef being hit by a car. In order to create more dramatic sound effects, or simply to record sound effects clearly, they are usually recorded separately, in a studio environment with no background sound or reverberation. There are also many collections of pre-recorded sound effects that are available to filmmakers.

During sound editing the dialogue, music and sound effects are edited into separate audio tracks. When the tracks are complete, a **sound mix** brings the various tracks together in a sound studio, editing program or audio mixing program. The levels of individual sounds can be raised or lowered in relation to the other sounds, while the character of each individual sound can be controlled and enhanced to create a rich, multi-layered soundtrack that complements the image.

While tracks can be built on fullcoat (16mm or 35mm) and a sound mix can be performed by playing each individual track on a separate playback machine while recording the mixed compilation of tracks on a fullcoat recorder, this kind of analog mixing is rarely done anymore. Instead almost all audio editing is done within digital systems, either using the audio controls of the editing software or exporting the audio to a dedicated audio program such as Digidesign's ProTools. Digital systems allow for very exact control of audio levels and they include a wide array of filters and controls to change the character of the sound.

If the movie will be finished on film, with an answer print and subsequent release prints, then the mixed track is used to make an optical soundtrack. In the optical track, the pattern of sounds becomes a pattern of dark lines on clear motion picture film. The optical track is printed onto the edge of the answer print. During projection, as light is shone through the optical track, this pattern of dark lines will dictate the voltage pattern sent to the speaker. The optical sound reader in a 16mm or 35mm projector will read the optical track from the edge of the print. Because film travels relatively slowly through a 16mm projector (36 feet per minute when projected at 24fps), optical sound on 16mm prints is very limited in quality. 35mm film moves much faster (90 feet per minute when projected at 24fps), and its optical sound quality is far superior.

Of course, productions that are finished following a completely digital workflow, and which will not be released on film, can be edited and mixed in an entirely digital environment. Though the ease of digital editing and mixing controls has led many filmmakers to mix their own films at home using editing software, often much better results can be obtained by having the mix done by an experienced sound engineer using dedicated audio equipment and software in an acoustically controlled environment. This makes it easier to put together a precisely designed soundtrack that combines with the visuals to create a quality film experience for the viewer.

Chapter 12

Distribution

For independent filmmakers the distribution and exhibition landscape has never been more complicated. The chances of a large number of people seeing your work have never been better, but generating significant revenue, especially from a short film, remains difficult. In addition to the traditional venues such as theatrical distribution (on film or video) and broadcast television, copies of films can be sold for home viewing and can be viewed on the web or on mobile devices such as tablets or smart phones. Most filmmakers will release their film on several or all of these platforms, giving different audiences many chances to see it instead of relying on a one-time theatrical release to reach a relatively small audience.

Film Prints

Movies that are finished on film go through a series of specific steps to get to the film print stage. A filmmaker might finish his or her film to a projection print for aesthetic reasons, but it has increasingly become the case that most films are finished on film to enhance their chances of gaining **theatrical exhibition**. Theatrical exhibition is the release of a film in movie theaters as opposed to other means of showing the film, such as home video, television or web-based exhibition. Theatrical exhibition is almost solely for feature-length films, so there are far fewer shorts finished on film today than there were in the past.

In order to make an answer print of a film the filmmaker must follow the proper procedures for matchback, conforming of the negative and creation of an optical soundtrack in order to prepare for striking prints. This process is discussed in Chapter 8, *Editing Mechanics* and Chapter 11, *Sound.*

There is a distinct advantage to having a 35mm print for film festivals, since many festivals exhibit 35mm in their biggest and best venues with the best sound systems. Consequently, it is not uncommon for a filmmaker who has made a film in 16mm or super-16 to create a 35mm blow-up of the film for festival exhibition. A blow-up is an enlargement from a smaller format to a larger one. There are three ways to make such a blow-up. The conventional method is to have the lab make a low contrast intermediate 35mm printing master of the film. An answer print with sound can be made from the intermediate. The film is ready for making multiple release prints if a distributor wants to acquire it and exhibit it theatrically.

An alternative to a conventional film blow-up is to take the film through the process of making a **digital intermediate**. A digital intermediate (**D.I.**) is a high-resolution scan of the film, made frame-by-frame to a digital file. The digital file can be manipulated in a great variety of ways before it is output to film again. The output is also a frame-by-frame high-resolution process, and the output can be to any format, so a film shot in 16mm or super-16 can be scanned to create a D.I. and then output to a 35mm intermediate that would be used to strike an answer print and any subsequent release prints. These methods of making a 35mm blow-up are quite expensive and beyond the budget of many filmmakers.

A third, somewhat less expensive, method to make a blow-up from 16mm is to make a one-time 35mm positive print directly from the 16mm negative. After the negative has been conformed, it is copied in an optical printer, directly to 35mm positive print stock. This single print can be used for festival screenings, but the film is not ready for making additional future prints without first going through one of the more conventional methods of creating an intermediate printing master. The single answer print made using this one-time method can cost one-third to one-fourth as much as going the standard route.

Film Festivals

Some of the first outlets many filmmakers pursue for a newly completed film are film festivals. There are thousands of film festivals in existence today, and most of them charge entry fees. Since there are so many film festivals to choose from, and because they cost money to enter and acceptance is often quite competitive, it is very important that a filmmaker does some research and homework before submitting a film.

Some festivals are primarily for feature-length films, and some are mainly for shorts. Some are looking for experimental works and others for narratives or documentaries. Some are strictly dedicated to animation. One way to begin to find out what a particular festival is all about is to check its website, but that doesn't always tell the whole story. At times, vague wording could encourage entries that are not a good fit.

Before entering a film festival it is a good idea to consider your own reasons for doing so. Maybe you simply want your new film to be seen by an audience. Maybe you want to get as much recognition for your new work as possible in hopes that the recognition will help you secure grant money or raise investment money for a future project. A filmmaker who has just completed a feature-length film might hope to use the festival route to try to secure a commercial **distribution deal**. A distribution deal involves selling the rights to market a film to a company that specializes in licensing movies to movie theaters, television outlets, for home video use or to any other potential venue for a finished film.

The nature of your film combined with your reasons for wanting to enter it into film festivals should help narrow the field of festivals to consider. Entering a narrative into a festival that is oriented to documentaries would be a waste of time and money. If you are looking for commercial distribution for a feature film, it would make sense to try to get it shown at festivals that are known to be frequented by representatives of distribution companies before sending it to festivals that are more oriented to film buffs.

There are a number of ways to investigate film festivals. There are books that are devoted to navigating the realm of festivals, but word-of-mouth from other filmmakers who have had experience at various festivals can be a valuable aid in figuring out which ones might be right for your new film. There are websites devoted to film festivals and even one, withoutabox.com, that allows a filmmaker to upload all of the relevant information about a film once and then enter individual film festivals with just a click (and payment of the entry fee to the festival). Film festivals that participate accept entries by accessing this uploaded information.

Distribution Deals

There are many different kinds of distribution deals that a filmmaker might encounter. Some distribution deals are actually made before production of the film begins, but that is seldom the case for an independent filmmaker working with a low budget. Anyone who has ever made a feature-length independent film hoped that a commercial distributor would recognize the potential of the newly completed movie and offer a lot of money for the right to distribute it to theaters. When a distributor offers up-front money for the right to distribute a film, that money is referred to as an **advance**.

Every so often there is a new success story that inspires many hopeful filmmakers. Films like *The Blair Witch Project* (1999) and *Paranormal Activity* (2007) come along now and then, and the makers of such movies receive lucrative advances from distributors who buy the rights to market the film. But there are thousands of other movies, some of them beautifully made, that never get any meaningful distribution offers. Distributors are in business to make money, and even an altruistic distribution company is not going to risk a lot of money on a film they are not sure they can sell. When an advance is made, the distribution company usually also offers the filmmaker a portion of future proceeds. The advance is discounted from any future proceeds before the filmmaker is entitled to additional funds.

A relatively common scenario for an independent feature filmmaker is an offer of a distribution contract that includes a very small advance or no advance at all. The distribution company offers to promote the film and promises a percentage of future "profits." Distribution companies, though, frequently use accounting methods that assign percentages of their corporate operating costs to various projects in a way that makes returns to most contracted artists unlikely. It would be foolish to sign a contract of any sort without hiring an entertainment lawyer to dissect it first. Regardless, many filmmakers are much more concerned with getting their film seen and establishing a reputation than with worrying about how much money they can make. If the main goal is to get the film seen and to gain wider recognition, it can make sense to accept a distribution deal that might not promise to be lucrative. It depends upon the filmmaker and the circumstances.

Distribution for short films is entirely different than feature film distribution. Commercial distributors rarely acquire short films because there are few opportunities to make money from them. Filmmakers seldom expect to make much money from a short. Shorts are often made purely for purposes of artistic expression, or they are made to serve as a "calling card" that showcases the filmmaker's talent in order to help in finding work or in finding funding for a new, often bigger, project. Makers of short films are typically more focused on simply finding outlets for their work. The outlets can include film festivals, group screenings at local venues, public access and local television showings and web-based exhibition.

There are a handful of organizations that specialize in distributing short films that are more oriented to a fine art approach to film and video. Canyon Cinema and The Film-Makers' Cooperative rent 16mm film prints, but they also deal with 35mm and even super-8 film rentals. In many cases they also sell DVDs of represented artists' works. Facets Multi-Media and the Video Data Bank specialize in the work of video artists, renting and selling tapes and dvds. There are other distributors of this kind around the world.

A filmmaker who is looking for distribution for art-oriented or experimental works, whether shorts or longer works, can contact these distributors directly.

Broadcast

While some television stations and networks air programs featuring independently produced films, broadcast television remains a difficult venue for independent and beginning filmmakers. Some PBS affiliates and some independent stations air programs consisting of locally produced films. PBS series like "POV" and "Nova" regularly feature the work of independent producers, and series like these may have an open application process with a selection committee that screens submissions. While some of the more prominent cable stations occasionally show programs that include the work of independent filmmakers, these stations typically prefer to deal only with distribution companies. Broadcasters usually pay for the broadcast rights to a film for a certain period of time.

Web Video

Many filmmakers post their work on-line. A video file uploaded to a site like YouTube or available for download from iTunes can be seen by millions of people around the world. Web video has become a distribution opportunity that is easy to implement and too ubiquitous to pass up. Many filmmakers use this opportunity to get their films seen by as many people as possible, and some hope that web notoriety will lead to greater support for future projects.

Since internet connections can only handle a relatively small flow of data, video files intended for presentation on the web must be small, measured in megabytes instead of gigabytes. The video files need to be compressed (See Chapter 3, *The Video Camera and Recorder*). This compression has a negative effect on image quality, so the trick to preparing a video file for the web is to make it as small as possible with as little effect on the image as possible. Most digital editing programs have several options and settings for creating web-ready video files.

Once a compressed video file has been created, there are two ways to make it available on the web. You can include a link to the file on your own personal website, or you can use aggregate sites such as YouTube, Vimeo, iTunes, or BitTorrent. The advantage of using your own site is that you can control the presentation of the film. Visitors to the site can be given information about the film, the makers, other films by the same people or any information that you want the viewer to have. The disadvantage is that you must design the website or pay someone else to do so, rent space on a web server and pay to own the unique name of the website. It may also be difficult to attract viewers to the site.

Aggregate video sites allow you to upload your file to their site, usually for free. Having many different videos in one place attracts many more viewers. The disadvantage is that the filmmaker has minimal control over the web page where the video is posted and the information contained on that web page. The most popular aggregate sites may also be too popular, and your dramatic narrative film may get lost in a sea of crashing skateboarders and cats playing the piano.

Once a film is on an aggregate site, though, links to it can be embedded in social networking sites, such as Facebook and Twitter, and the video page itself can link to your own personal website if you have one. Aggregate sites such as iTunes also allow people to download your film to their iPods, tablets and smart phones, and of course these mobile devices can browse to a site such as YouTube. Overall, having your film on an aggregate video site will make it possible for millions of people to see it, often many times. For that very reason, many film festivals only accept films that haven't yet been available on the web.

Distribution on Optical Discs

Optical discs are small plastic discs that contain data in the form of small "pits" in the plastic or patterns of dye on the plastic. These pits and patterns are read as 1s and 0s by a laser. The most common optical discs that store video information are **DVD-ROM** (Digital Versatile Disc – Read Only Memory), **BD-R** (Blu-ray Disc – Recordable), **DVD-Video** and **Blu-ray** discs. DVDs use a red laser and can hold anywhere from 4 GB to 18 GB of data. Blu-ray discs use a blue laser, which (because blue has a shorter wavelength than red) is finer and can read and write much more information on the same size disc (from 25GB to over 100GB). Because DVD discs were invented first, devices that can play Blu-ray discs can play DVDs, but devices designed to play DVDs cannot play Blu-ray discs.

DVD-ROM and BD-R discs are usually used to transfer digital data between computers. A video file on one of these discs would be similar to those used for viewing on the web, but it would usually be larger and of higher quality. Such files can only be viewed on a computer with the proper video player software, usually after being copied to the computer's hard drive.

DVD-Video and Blu-ray discs hold specially-formatted video and audio files. The discs can be played on most computers, but they can also be played on stand-alone players and game consoles. In addition to including one or several films, these discs often have other "special features" and interactive menus to help the viewer navigate between them. Creating the specially-formatted files and designing menus and features can be a complex process that involves much more than copying a video file to a disc. Often special "authoring" software is needed and discs meant for large-scale commercial distribution need to be duplicated in a special facility.

For films that were originally exhibited theatrically or on TV, distribution on optical discs is a second opportunity to gain viewers and make money, often more than the original exhibition garnered. For many low-budget filmmakers, DVD-Video or Blu-ray discs are the primary mode of distribution. Self-distributing these discs often takes a lot of marketing effort. In addition to having a website where the disc is offered for sale, copies are often sold by sites like

Amazon.com on a consignment basis: the filmmaker sends several copies to the seller and only receives payment for any copies that are sold. Only if all copies are sold out does the seller order more copies.

Social sites such as Twitter and Facebook are indispensable methods of free or cheap advertising for a DVD or Blu-ray release. Self-distributing filmmakers often hold "release party" live events that attract a crowd that would be likely to purchase the disc, such as holding a release party at a skate park for a skateboarding DVD or holding a live concert featuring a band that performs on the movie's soundtrack. For an independent filmmaker without a large marketing budget, selling enough optical discs to generate significant revenue can be very difficult and time-consuming.

Music Rights

Most films include some music within their soundtrack. There are times when a filmmaker might want to use published music as part of a soundtrack. Whether the music is popular and widely known or not, any music that is protected by copyright must be licensed before it can be used if the filmmaker intends to find distribution.

While it can be possible to license the rights to popular music, as is often done in feature films with significant budgets, it can be a complex and expensive process. Usually, two sets of rights have to be obtained. The **publishing rights** are typically held by the writer of the music (or their representative), while the **synchronization rights** are usually held by the company that put out the recording of the music. The publishing rights can be thought of as the intellectual property, the musical composition itself. These rights are sometimes easier to negotiate than the synchronization rights, the right to use the actual recording of the music, which is usually controlled by a corporation.

Some music is available without paying a licensing fee for the rights. In the United States music that was published prior to 1923 is no longer protected. Some music that has not had its copyright renewed might also be unprotected, and there is some music that was published without ever being copyrighted. Such "public domain" music is not protected and can be used without licensing. However, individual recordings of such music are usually protected, with rights for a particular performance belonging to the recording artist who has filed a copyright for their performance. If you hope to get wide exposure for a film, it is important to find a source of music that is legally available for free or to license the rights to the music you want to use.

There are also many sources for royalty-free recordings of music. Whether it means buying a cd or downloading files (usually, for a small one-time fee), this music has been created or cleared for use, and there are no big fees to pay or future royalty payments to worry about. The downside is that royalty-free music can sound generic.

It is often best to find an artist who will compose and record original music for a film, with the filmmaker and the composer making a mutually agreeable deal regarding the music rights and clearly securing the right to use that music. Such agreements should be in the form of a written contract in order to avoid any future misunderstandings or disagreements.

Promotion

Production stills are photographs taken on a film set for publicity and marketing purposes. For big-budget features, a photographer is usually present to take photographs during rehearsals or during actual takes. Sometimes production stills are posed on the set and may be shot between takes or when shooting for the day is completed. Because of this, production stills are often shots that do not exist in the film itself.

Even when shooting a low-budget film it is important to get good production stills for promotional purposes, including web sites, posters, film festival applications, press kits and DVD cover art. A filmmaker might designate a member of the crew to take photographs during shooting or, if the budget allows, hire a photographer for some of the shooting days. Using a frame of the film or a screen capture rarely results in a high-quality image. Good production stills can be the difference between a professional-looking promotional campaign and one that looks like an afterthought.

Trailers are commercials for films. Originally trailers were shown in movie theaters after the feature film for the purpose of marketing upcoming movies at that theater. Realizing that most of the patrons were leaving during the end credits of the feature and missing the trailers, theater operators began showing trailers to the captive audience *before* the movie. Because trailers are now screened in theaters before the film, they are also referred to as *previews*. Today, trailers are shown not only in theaters, but also on television and on-line, and they are frequently included on DVDs.

Trailers are usually created using footage taken from the film. The footage is edited into a short, attention-grabbing advertisement for the movie. Often voice-over narration or titles are used within the trailer. Movie trailers are edited from the most visually interesting, funny or exciting moments in the film. A well-made trailer should capture the interest of the audience without giving away too much of the plot. Most trailers for feature-length films are two-and-a-half minutes long. A trailer for a short film should probably be a minute or less in length.

Sometimes footage is shot specifically to create a trailer. Very short teaser trailers are made to create "buzz" about a film well in advance of its intended release. For the film *Cloverfield* (2008), producer J.J. Abrams created a teaser trailer before production of the movie began. The trailer did not include much information about the film. The trailer, like the film, was shot with a hand-held digital camera. It appeared to be footage from a New Years' Eve party. The party is interrupted by an explosion in lower Manhattan, and the trailer ends with the head of the Statue of Liberty landing in the street. The trailer did not include the title of the film; it gave just the name of the film's producer and its release date.

The distribution landscape is constantly changing, but the thing that won't change is that distributing and promoting a film will always take a lot of time and effort. The goal is to make sure that as many people see your film as possible, and that was the reason for all the time and effort you put into the film in the first place.

Glossary

2:3 pulldown: a type of pulldown that coverts four film frames into five frames of video, changing the frame rate from 24fps to 30fps on videotape. Using 2:3 pulldown, the film is also slowed down by 0.1% during transfer resulting in video that runs 29.97fps.

8mm: film **format** in which the strip of film is 8 millimeters wide.

16mm: film **format** in which the strip of film is 16 millimeters wide.

18% gray: a shade of gray that reflects 18% of the light hitting it; the standard that light metering systems are based upon; same as **medium gray.**

35mm: film **format** in which the strip of film is 35 millimeters wide.

180-degree rule: rule governing the concept of **screen direction**. When a 180-degree line or axis is established within a scene, all shots must be taken from one side of the line in order to ensure proper screen direction.

180-degree shutter: a shutter with an opening that is a half circle of metal, or 180 degrees.

720p: a **high-definition** video format that uses 720 horizontal lines of 1280 **pixels** each in a **progressive** frame.

1080i: an **HD** video format that uses 1080 horizontal lines of 1920 **pixels** each in an **interlaced** frame.

1080p: an **HD** video format that uses 1080 horizontal lines of 1920 **pixels** each in a **progressive** frame.

A-D converter: see **analog-to-digital converter**.

Additive primary colors: red, green and blue; the colors of light that when added together in equal amounts make white light.

Advance: up-front money that a distributor offers for the right to distribute a film. The advance is guaranteed money.

Amplitude: the volume or loudness of a sound.

Analog: a type of video or audio recording in which the charges on the **videotape** are a direct analog to the voltage signal from the **CCD**.

Analog-to-digital converter: converts information into a series of numbers for use in a digital device or a computer; **A-D converter**.

Animation: creating the illusion of motion where none exists by shooting objects or a sequence of drawings frame by frame with slight changes between frames.

Answer print: the first complete, finished print of a film, usually with sound.

Aperture: 1) in a film camera, the opening cut into the **aperture** plate which defines the edges of the frame. 2) in the lens, the adjustable **iris.**

Aperture plate: a metal plate in a film camera between the film and the lens. A frame sized cut-out in the plate defines the edges of the frame and allows light to strike the film.

ASA: American Standards Association; the scale which assigns a numerical rating to the speed, or sensitivity, of a film stock. ASA is interchangeable with **EI** and **ISO**.

Aspect ratio: the dimensions of the frame in a given **format**, described as a numerical ratio of the frame's width to its height. 16mm, 8mm and super-8 film all use an aspect ratio of 1.33:1; HD video has an aspect ration of 16:9.

Assembly: initial editing together of selected shots; the first step in the editing process.

Autofocus: a feature on most video cameras in which a sensor in the lens estimates distances to the object in the center of the frame and focuses to that distance.

Background light: a light that illuminates the background behind the subject.

Back light: light that hits a subject from behind. It doesn't usually serve as a significant source of illumination. Rather, its purpose is to outline the subject and separate it from its background.

Barndoors: hinged metal flaps that mount on the front of a light and which shape the light coming from the lighting unit.

Barrel: of the lens; the tube that connects and holds the lens **elements** in place.

Base: the flexible strip of **cellulose triacetate** material that the **emulsion** is coated onto.

Bass: low-frequency sound.

BD-R: Blu-ray Disc – Recordable; a common format of optical disc, typically used to transfer digital data between computers.

Binary: a number system in which any number is made up of a string of digits, and each digit can have one of only two values: 0 or 1.

Bit: a single digit in a **binary** number.

Bit depth: same as **bit rate**.

Bit rate: the number of possible values used to record each **sample** in a digital device; the higher the bit rate the greater the accuracy.

Black-and-white: a film stock that does not differentiate between colors; everything is reproduced in varying shades of gray from black to white.

Blocking: the choreographing of all movement in a shot, both subject movement within the frame and camera movement.

Blow-up: the process of rephotographing one film **format** onto another, larger film format.

Blu-ray: a common format of optical disc, Blu-ray discs hold specially-formatted video and audio files. The discs can be played on some computers, and they can also be played on stand-alone players and game consoles that use Blu-ray technology.

Boom: a pole used to hold a microphone so that it is as close as possible to the sound being recorded.

Bounce card: a large sheet of reflective material used to soften and direct light toward a subject when the light is "bounced" (or reflected).

Cable sync: a method of synchronizing sound and image in double-system film shooting. The camera and recorder are linked by a cable.

Camcorder: a machine that combines a video camera and recorder in one unit.

Camera gate: the area inside the camera in which the film is exposed to light.

Camera original: the film stock that has actually run through the camera. It can be negative or reversal.

Camera speed: same as **frame rate**.

Camera take: during shooting, a shot; the series of **frames** from camera start to camera stop; also simply called a **take**.

Cardioid microphone: a microphone which picks up sounds coming from its front and sides more clearly than it picks up sounds coming from behind.

Cathode ray tube: (**CRT**)a television monitor that creates an image by firing electrons at a phosphor-coated screen.

CCD: see **charge-coupled device**.

Cellulose triacetate: the flexible material that the film **base** is made of.

Changing bag: a portable light-tight bag that is used for loading film stock into a camera (a portable "darkroom").

Changing tent: like a **changing bag** but supported by a rigid frame for ease of use.

Charge-coupled device: (**CCD**) the chip in some video cameras that changes light values into electrical voltage.

Chrominance: the color information in a video signal.

Clip: in a **non-linear editing** system a set of directions that tell the computer which portion of a **media file** to play.

Clones: digital video or audio files made by copying digital data from one machine to another with no **generational loss**.

Close-up: (**CU**) when of a person, usually a shot of the head and shoulders.

CMOS: see **Complementary Metal Oxide Semiconductor**.

Codec: the series of algorithms that control *co*mpression and *dec*ompression of digital information.

Color temperature: a measure in **Kelvins** (K) of the color quality of a light source. Lower color temperatures indicate the red/orange part of the spectrum, while higher color temperatures tend toward blue.

Compact Flash card: a type of memory card commonly used for data storage in digital audio recorders and some video cameras.

Complementary Metal Oxide Semiconductor: (**CMOS**) the chip in some video cameras that changes light values into electrical voltage and converts that voltage into **binary** numbers.

Component: a video signal that separates **luminance** and **chrominance** information, and breaks the chrominance information into two separate signals as well.

Composite: a video signal that combines **luminance** and **chrominance** information into one signal.

Composite shot: a visual effect created by combining elements of several shots into one image.

Compression: reduction of the size and quality of digitized files in order to conserve space on a computer's hard drive.

Condenser microphone: a microphone that uses a power source to boost or amplify the audio signal.

Conforming: the process of editing the **camera original** to match the edited **workprint** or digital off-line edit frame for frame.

Continuity: maintaining believable spatial and temporal relationships within a scene. Preserving continuity involves maintaining proper **screen direction**, positioning and timing so that a series of shots showing pieces of an action fit together in a natural and seamless way.

Continuity editing: editing a sequence of shots to create a scene in which time and space seem to be uninterrupted; also called "cutting for continuity."

Contrast range: for a video camera or film stock, the range from the darkest image that can be recorded to the brightest that can be handled. For a shot, the range from the darkest shadow to the brightest highlight.

Core: a plastic hub that **16mm** (and **35mm**) **camera original** film is wound on, usually in longer lengths (400 feet or more). Cores are also used to store film during editing.

Cross-lighting: a lighting arrangement in which two lights are positioned so that their beams cut across each other in an "X." Frequently, this type of set-up is used so that each light can do double duty, serving as a **key light** on one subject and a **back light** on another simultaneously.

CRT: see **Cathode Ray Tube**.

Crystal sync: a method of synchronizing sound and image in double-system film shooting. The camera's speed is controlled by a crystal oscillator while a crystal in the analog recorder generates a sync pulse.

CU: see **close-up**.

Cut: point where a shot begins or ends; the point at which two shots are edited together.

Cutaway: a shot related to but not directly a part of the main action within a sequence. Cutaway shots can emphasize important details and also allow greater flexibility in editing.

D-A converter: see **digital-to-analog converter.**

Dailies: unedited footage; same as **rushes**.

DAT: see **Digital Audio Tape**.

Datacine: a device used to electronically convert film to a digital file.

Day-for-night: an often unconvincing technique of shooting night scenes in daylight.

Daylight-balanced: 1) in the case of a light source, one which emits light of the "daylight" **color temperature** (5500 K). 2) in the case of a color film stock, one which is manufactured to reproduce color correctly when exposed under illumination of the "daylight" color temperature.

Daylight-blue gel: same as **full-blue gel**.

Daylight spool: a black metal spool with solid sides that **16mm** (and sometimes **35mm**) **camera original** film is wound on for loading into a camera in low light.

Decibel: a measure of the **amplitude** of a sound.

Decompression: the decoding of a compressed digital file.

Depth of field: the area in front of and behind the **plane of critical focus** in which objects appear to be in focus.

D.I.: see **digital intermediate**.

Digital: a system in which information is stored as **binary** numbers.

Digital Audio Tape: (**DAT**) an audio recording format in which sound information is recorded onto **magnetic tape** as a series of number values.

Digital intermediate: (**D.I.**) a high-resolution scan of a film, made frame-by-frame to a digital file. The digital file can be manipulated in a great variety of ways before it is output at high resolution to film again.

Digital-to-analog converter: in a digital device, converts a series of binary numbers into sound or picture information; **D-A converter**.

Digitize: the process of converting **analog** material into digital files.

DIN: Deutsche Industrie Norm; European standard for rating film sensitivity. This scale is not interchangeable with **ASA**, **EI** or **ISO**.

Dissolve: an on-screen transition in which it appears as if one image gradually blends into another image; a **fade-out** simultaneously occurring over a **fade-in**.

Distribution deal: selling the rights to market a film to a company that specializes in licensing movies to movie theaters, television outlets, for home video use or to any other potential venue for a finished film.

Documentary: a style of filmmaking which attempts to record some aspect of real life.

Dolly: 1) a wheeled support on which the camera rests. 2) the camera movement that results when a dolly is moved.

Double-perf film: a strip of film with **sprocket holes** along both edges.

Double-system sound: a type of filmmaking in which picture and sound are captured at the same time but on separate machines.

Dubbing: copying an **analog** audio tape or **videotape**.

Dusk-for-night: a technique of shooting night scenes during the brief dusk period after the sun has moved below the horizon but while there is still sufficient light from the sky.

Dutch angle: a shot composed so that the image is tilted in the frame.

DVD-ROM: Digital Versatile Disc – Read Only Memory; a common format of optical disc, typically used to transfer digital data between computers.

DVD-Video: a common format of optical disc, DVDs can hold anywhere from 4 GB to 18 GB of specially-formatted video and audio files. The discs can be played on most computers, but they can also be played on stand-alone players and game consoles.

Dynamic microphone: a microphone that does not use a power source to boost its signal.

Dynamic range: of a sound receiving device, the range from the softest sound it can register to the loudest it can handle; of a sound producing device, the range from the softest to loudest sound produced.

ECU: see **extreme close-up**.

Edit controller: in a **linear editing system** a device that connects to the source and record decks and controls the recording of material from one tape onto another tape.

Edit-decision list: (**EDL**) a printout of every shot in an edited tape usually consisting of **SMPTE time code** numbers, used to create the final, on-line edit of the video.

Editing: process of cutting together various shots to create scenes or sequences.

Editing suite: a room designed for video editing, outfitted with the necessary computers, decks, mixers and any other equipment necessary for editing.

EDL: see **Edit-decision list**.

EI: Exposure Index; a scale indicating film speed, or sensitivity, which is interchangeable with **ASA** or **ISO** for film stocks. EI 100 is the same as ASA 100 or ISO 100.

Element: a precision-ground piece of glass in a lens.

ELS: see **extreme long shot**.

Emulsion: a gelatin suspension of light sensitive **grains** of silver compounds spread on one side of the film's **base**.

Envelope: the glass covering of a **lamp** or light bulb.

Erase head: part of a recorder that produces a constant magnetic field which destroys any previously existing signal on a tape.

Establishing shot: a shot that shows the physical space, defining spatial relationships within the scene; usually a **long shot** or an **extreme long shot**.

Experimental: a type of film that is often more concerned with the graphic or structural elements of film than it is with telling a story or documenting real life. Experimental film is a catch-all phrase that is frequently used to describe any abstract, non-narrative or other unusual approach.

Extreme close-up: (**ECU**) a shot in which a small detail of a person or object fills the frame.

Extreme long shot: (**ELS**) a shot that shows a large area of the physical environment.

Fade-in: an on-screen transition in which an image gradually appears out of a blank (usually black) screen.

Fade-out: an on-screen transition in which an image at full value gradually diminishes into a blank (usually black) screen.

Fall-off: the lessening in intensity of light falling on a subject as the subject moves farther from the light source.

Fast: 1) in a film stock, one with larger grain and, therefore, greater sensitivity to light. 2) in a lens, one with a large maximum **iris** opening, making it capable of shooting in low-light situations.

Fast motion: accelerated action created by running the camera at a slower **frame rate** than the viewing speed. It is also known as **undercranking.**

Feed reel: a reel on which film is stored before it is run through a camera or projector.

Fields: electronic horizontal lines that make up half of the information in an **interlaced** video frame. One video frame is comprised of two fields.

Filament: in a **lamp**, a small thread of tungsten that glows when heated, creating the lamp's light.

Fill light: light used to illuminate shadow areas and to control the **lighting contrast ratio**. The fill light is almost always a soft light source.

Film chain: a device for transferring film to video using a video camera and a film projector with a mirror set at a 45-degree angle between them.

Film plane: the plane in which the film travels as it runs through the **camera gate** where it is exposed; should coincide with the **focal plane**.

Filter: 1) a piece of colored glass or gelatin that changes the characteristics of light passing through it. 2) in video, a kind of effect that alters color, brightness or other characteristics of the video signal.

Filter switch: on a **super-8** camera, a switch that inserts or retracts (between the lens and the film) the orange **filter** that corrects the color of daylight when shooting on **tungsten-balanced** film.

Fine cut: final stage in the editing process in which pacing and rhythm have been refined.

Fisheye lens: an extreme **wide-angle lens** that exaggerates depth and causes horizontal lines to bend.

Flicker fusion: a physiological phenomenon. If an image is presented to the human eye, removed and returned quickly enough, the human eye and brain see the image as being constant.

Focal length: the "size" of a lens, usually expressed in millimeters; the distance from the optical center of a lens to the focal plane.

Focal plane: the plane onto which the lens focuses rays of light; should coincide with the **film plane** in a film camera or the video chip in a video camera.

Focusing ring: a ring on a lens that indicates (and focuses the lens for) the distance between the **focal plane** and the **plane of critical focus**.

Footcandle: a standard unit of light measurement. Footcandles can be measured with **incident light meters** but not with **reflected light meters.**

Format: the gauge or width of a film stock (35mm, 16mm, 8mm, super-8, etc.) or a specific type of video (720p, 1080i, 480i, etc.).

fps: frames per second.

Frame: 1) one single image on a strip of film or in a video. 2) the edges of the image as seen in the viewfinder or on the screen.

Frame rate: the speed at which video is shot or at which film runs through the camera, measured in frames per second (**fps**).

Frequency: a measure of how many cycles of a sound wave pass a certain point in a given time period. A large object vibrates slowly, producing a low-frequency sound, while a small object vibrates more quickly, producing a high-frequency sound.

Frequency range: the range from the lowest to the highest frequencies a sound receiver can register or which a sound producer can create.

f-stop: a number that indicates the diameter of the opening of the lens **iris** and therefore indicates the amount of light that it lets in.

Full-blue gel: a sheet of color-correcting acetate used to convert a **tungsten-balanced** movie light to the daylight **color temperature**.

Gain: the strength of a video or audio voltage signal.

Generational loss: when film is printed or **analog** tape is **dubbed** the image is degraded.

Grains: photosensitive crystals of silver halides that are suspended in the gelatin of a film **emulsion**.

Gray card: a rectangular piece of cardboard that is dyed a specific shade of gray on one side. A gray card reflects 18 percent of the light that hits it. It is neutral in tone, with no color bias.

Handheld: shooting without using a tripod or other support. The cameraperson holds the camera.

HD: see **high-definition** video.

HDMI: see **High-Definition Multimedia Interface**.

Head: the beginning of a reel of film.

Head drum: a cylindrical rotating drum in a video recorder that contains multiple **record heads**, **erase heads** and **playback heads**.

Head room: allowing appropriate compositional space above a subject's head.

Helical scan: the diagonal path of magnetized particles on **videotape** after the tape has passed the **head drum** during recording.

Hertz: (**Hz**) a unit used to measure a sound's **frequency**; also sometimes called "cycles per second."

High angle shot: a shot taken with the camera at an angle above the subject.

High-definition: (**HD**) video **formats** with at least 720 horizontal lines.

High-Definition Multimedia Interface: (**HDMI**) a video cable that can carry an uncompressed, high-quality video signal along with several audio channels.

Highlight: the brightest area of an illuminated object.

Hypercardioid microphone: a microphone which picks up sounds coming from the front of the microphone more clearly than sounds coming from beside or behind it; same as **supercardioid microphone**.

Hz: see **Hertz**.

Imax: a film format shot on 65mm film with an extremely large frame size.

Incandescent lamp: a type of lamp that produces light by heating a tungsten filament.

Incident light meter: a meter that measures the amount of light falling on the subject.

In focus: rendered sharp by a lens.

Intensity: brightness of a light source.

Interlaced: a method of creating a video **frame** out of two **fields**, each containing alternating lines of the frame.

Intermittent movement: 1) the mechanism that moves the film through the camera or projector gate in a stop-and-start fashion so that each frame is stationary during the moment of exposure or projection; 2) the action of the **pull-down claw**.

Iris: an adjustable metal diaphragm inside a lens that can be opened or closed to control the amount of light reaching the film or the video chip.

ISO: International Standards Organization; a widely used scale indicating film speed or sensitivity, which is interchangeable with **ASA** and **EI**. ISO 100 is the same as ASA 100 or EI 100.

Jump cut: a visually jarring edit that disrupts continuity.

Kelvins: the scale used for color temperature.

Keycode: a machine-readable bar code form of **latent edge number** information.

Key light: the primary source of illumination in a lighting set-up.

kHz: see **kiloHertz**.

KiloHertz: (**kHz**) thousands of cycles per second; used to measure sound **frequency** or the **sampling rate** of a digital device.

Lamp: the bulb in a lighting unit.

Latent edge numbers: numbers printed along one edge of **16mm** and **35mm** film stock; used to match an edited **workprint** or a digital edit to the **camera original** during **conforming**.

Latent image: the invisible (or potential) image formed on film when it is initially exposed to light, but before it has been processed.

Latitude: the amount of overexposure and underexposure a film stock is capable of without losing detail. Latitude is greater in negative film than in reversal film.

Lavaliere microphone: a very small microphone that can be clipped to an actor's clothing or hidden on the set.

Leader: film, usually white, black or clear, that is spliced at the **head** and **tail** of a reel of film to protect the footage and allow for labeling. Leader can be used within the body of an edited film to create a black screen, clear screen, etc.

Leading the action: composing a moving object within the frame with more space in front of the object (in the direction it is moving) than behind it.

Lighting contrast ratio: a measure of the difference in light intensity between the lighter and darker sides of a subject. It is written as a numerical ratio such as 2:1.

Linear editing system: a video editing system that uses multiple videotape decks to re-record material to new tapes in a new order.

Long lens: same as **telephoto lens**.

Long shot: (**LS**) in the case of a shot of a person, the whole person is shown from head to toe.

Long take: a style of filmmaking that emphasizes long, uninterrupted shots.

Loop: a small amount of slack in a strip of film between the constantly moving **sprocket wheel** and the **intermittent movement** in the camera or projector gate.

Low angle shot: a shot taken with the camera at an angle below the subject.

Lower thirds: an on-screen title near the bottom of the frame.

LS: see **long shot**.

Luminance: the brightness information in a video signal.

Macro lens: a lens capable of shooting **extreme close-ups** by focusing on very close objects. Usually a macro lens can focus as close as a few inches.

Magnetic fullcoat: thick magnetic tape sprocketed like film and available in the same gauges as film.

Master shot: a single shot of an entire action, usually taken with a wide field of view.

Master tape: the final, high-quality version of the film created in an **on-line edit**. Duplicates are made from the master tape.

Matchback: the process of matching **camera original** film footage to an edit made on a computerized editing system.

Match cut: a smooth edit that maintains the continuity of action from one shot to the next, creating the illusion of continuous motion.

MCU: see **medium close-up**.

Media files: digitized video; the actual set of 1s and 0s that make up the audio and video information.

Medium close-up: (**MCU**) a shot in which the size of the subject is between that of a **medium shot** and a **close-up**.

Medium gray: same as **18% gray**.

Medium long shot: (**MLS**) a shot in which the size of the subject is between that of a **medium shot** and a **long shot**.

Medium shot: (**MS**) in the case of a person, frequently it is a shot framing the person from the waist up.

Megahertz: (**MHz**) millions of times per second; a measure of the **sampling rate** of a digital device.

Menu: text displayed in the viewfinder of a video camera that shows the various controls, the options for each control and the options currently selected for each one.

MHz: see **Megahertz**.

Microphone: a mechanical device that captures sound and converts it into a voltage signal.

MLS: see **medium long shot**.

Montage: editing technique in which shots are cut together without concern for continuity. The juxtaposition of many shots creates meaning that the individual shots cannot convey alone.

Motion blur: the blurring of a moving object on a film or video image; a slower **shutter speed** results in more motion blur.

Motion effects: video effects in which the video frame is moved, resized, rotated or distorted.

Motivated light: light with a source of origin that is shown or suggested within the scene.

MS: see **medium shot**.

Narrative: a style of filmmaking that tells a story.

National Television System Committee: (**NTSC**) the video standard used in North America.

Neutral angle: a shot taken on the 180-degree line; a shot with neutral screen direction, favoring neither screen left nor screen right.

Neutral gray: same as **18% gray**.

Night-for-night: a technique of shooting outdoor night scenes at night while using lighting units to selectively illuminate and highlight.

Non-destructive editing: a method of editing on a computer where the source material is not altered during the editing process.

Non-linear editing system: an editing system that uses a computer's random access capability and software to manipulate digitized video with no loss of quality.

NTSC: see **National Television System Committee**.

Off-line clips: a set of instructions that refer to missing **media files**.

Off-line editing: the process of editing in a lower-quality **format** in order to create an **edit decision list** for **on-line editing**.

Omnidirectional microphone: a microphone that picks up sounds equally well from all directions.

Omnimax: a film format shot on 65mm film with an extremely large frame size, projected onto a curved screen.

One-chip camera: a video cameras that uses a single **CCD** or **CMOS** to record the image.

On-line editing: usually the final stage of editing in which the high-quality version of the edited film is created from an **edit-decision list**.

Open up: to open the lens **iris** in order to let more light pass through.

Out of focus: the image is not sharp.

Outtakes: shots that are not selected for inclusion in the edited film.

Overexpose: to allow too much light to hit the film or the video chip.

Overlapping action: a shooting technique in which an action is repeated while being shot multiple times from a variety of camera angles; used to create **match cuts**.

Oxide: magnetically sensitive material used in **videotape**, audio tape and magnetic fullcoat.

Pan: a camera movement in which the camera is pivoted along its horizontal axis.

Parallel editing: editing back and forth between two or more scenes to indicate that they are occurring simultaneously.

Perforations: same as **sprocket holes**.

Persistence of vision: when a series of drawings or photographs of an object in motion are viewed in rapid succession, each image is briefly retained by the retina and the brain blends the individual pictures together, creating the illusion of motion.

Pick-up pattern: a microphone's directional characteristics for gathering sound.

Pixels: the small rectangles or squares that make up the image on a television monitor.

Plane of critical focus: the plane in which all objects are in sharpest focus. It is parallel to the focal plane and its distance from the **focal plane** is determined by the distance set on the **focusing ring**.

Playback head: the part of a recorder that reads the signal stored on a tape.

Positive print: a film copy of a negative image in which brightness and color values are the opposite of those in the negative. In a positive print values are the same as what was seen through the viewfinder during original photography.

Post-dubbed sound: sound that is added to a film in post-production.

Pressure plate: a spring-loaded plate in a motion picture camera that holds the film flat against the **aperture plate** in the camera.

Prime lens: a lens with a single, fixed **focal length**.

Processing: running exposed film through chemicals that develop and fix the **latent image**, making it a visible, permanent image.

Production stills: photographs taken on a film set for publicity and marketing purposes.

Production value: the overall look of a film, or those elements that affect the look of the film such as locations, lighting, sets, props, acting, etc.

Progressive: a video **frame** that is not divided into **fields** like an **interlaced** frame.

Proposal: written statement of a film's concept; usually the first step in the scripting process.

Publishing rights: in a musical composition, publishing rights are the intellectual property (the composition itself), the rights to use the musical composition are typically held by the writer of the music (or their representative).

Pulldown: a film-to-videotape transfer method that compensates for the difference between film and video frame rates.

Pull-down claw: the pin or claw that engages a **perforation** of the film and advances it one frame, while the **shutter** blocks light from the moving film.

Pull focus: changing focus during a shot in order to keep a moving object in focus.

Quality: of a light source; a primary characteristic of light, broadly defined as being either hard or soft.

Quartz-halogen lamp: a tungsten lamp with a glass **envelope** made of quartz glass and with halogen gas inside the glass envelope; quartz-halogen lamps create far more light intensity for their size than standard **incandescent lamps**.

Rack focus: shifting focus during a shot in order to direct attention from one area of the frame to another.

Raster: the pattern of lines that make the image on a **cathode ray tube** monitor.

Record deck: in a **linear editing system**, the video deck that records parts of the source tape onto a new tape

Record head: the part of a recorder that encodes the video or audio signal onto magnetic tape.

Reflected light meter: a meter that measures the amount of light reflected by a subject.

Reflector: the scoop-shaped part of a lighting unit that directs the beam of light in one general direction.

Registration pin: a pin that engages a **sprocket hole** during exposure, holding the film perfectly still.

Release print: projection print of a film made from the **camera original** and incorporating all timing changes approved in the **answer print**.

Render file: a **media file** that is created in the editing system that incorporates a video effect and that can be played back in real time.

Reverse telecine: the process of reversing the **2:3 pulldown** from film that has been transferred to video, restoring it to its original 24fps frame rate.

Rough cut: intermediate editing stage in which shots are edited and re-edited until the footage is refined into a **fine cut**.

Rule of Thirds: a compositional guideline in which the frame is divided into thirds horizontally and vertically with important objects positioned at the intersection of the dividing lines.

Running time: the total time of the film, from beginning to end.

Rushes: unedited footage; same as **dailies**.

Sampling rate: the number of times per second a digital device checks incoming information and converts it into **binary** numbers.

Scene: a **narrative** film is divided into a series of scenes, each usually consisting of an event that takes place during a continuous period of time in a single location.

Screen direction: the direction a character or object is facing or the direction of movement within a shot. Screen direction is usually described as being **screen left**, **screen right** or neutral.

Screen left/screen right: an indication of **screen direction** or position. A character positioned on the left side of the frame, as seen through the camera and on the screen, is said to be screen left. That same character, if facing the other side of the frame, would be said to be facing screen right.

Screenplay: same as **script**.

Script: written scenes for a film describing relevant action and dialogue, usually following a specific format.

Script breakdown: an organized listing of the various details within a **script**, such as actors, locations and props; used to gather and organize the necessary elements for each shooting day.

SD: see **standard-definition** video.

Shadow: the darker area of an illuminated object or frame.

Shooting plan: a list grouping similar shots together so that all the shots with the same camera position and lighting set-up are shot at once, allowing for economical use of shooting time.

Shooting script: chronological list describing each **shot** within a **scene** or an entire film in terms of image size, camera angle and camera movement.

Short lens: same as **wide-angle lens**.

Short-range motion phenomenon: a physiological phenomenon. If a series of fixed images are projected onto a screen in succession, with slight differences between them, the illusion of movement can be created on the screen.

Shot: a continuous series of frames unbroken by a cut or by turning the cameras off; one **camera take**.

Shotgun microphone: a microphone with a narrowly directional **pick-up pattern** that picks up sounds coming from the front of the microphone more clearly than sound coming from beside or behind it; the common usage term for **hypercardioid** or **supercardioid** microphones.

Shutter: a metal disk that spins in front of the **aperture** of a film camera. Part of the disk is cut away so that when the film is in motion the metal prevents light from reaching the film. When the film is motionless the cut-out portion of the disk allows light to expose a frame.

Shutter angle: the size, measured in degrees, of the camera's **shutter opening**.

Shutter opening: the cut-out portion of the shutter which allows light to expose a frame. The angle (in degrees) of the shutter opening and the **frame rate** of the camera determine the **shutter speed**.

Shutter speed: the amount of time that light hits each frame.

Single-channel video: video displayed as a single image, projected or on a monitor.

Single-perf film: a strip of film with **sprocket holes** along only one edge.

Single-system sound: a method of shooting sync sound in which picture and sound are captured by the same device at the same time.

Slate: a black or white board with sticks that can be clapped together in front of the camera, with both the camera and the audio recorder running, at the beginning of every **take**. The editor uses the slate to put shots in sync.

Slow: 1) in a film stock, one with smaller grain and therefore, less sensitivity to light. 2) in a lens, one with a relatively small maximum **iris** opening.

SMPTE time code: a series of numbers developed by the Society of Motion Picture and Television Engineers that identifies individual video frames and allows videotape and computerized editing to be frame-exact.

Socket: the part of a lighting unit that holds the **lamp**.

Soft light: a quality of light that is characterized by diffused lighting and indistinct shadows.

Sound effects: sounds on a film **soundtrack** (such as footsteps, traffic noise, a doorbell, etc.) which are not music or speech.

Sound mix: the process of recording edited tracks together onto a single, uncut track. The level and character of each individual sound can be controlled to create a multi-layered **soundtrack**.

Soundtrack: the aural accompaniment to a film.

Source deck: in an editing system, the **video deck** that plays the original material.

Spatial compression: a type of video **compression** that keeps all the video frames but removes some information from each frame.

Speed: a measure of the film's sensitivity to light in **ASA**, **ISO** or **EI**; a **fast** film is more sensitive (and requires less light) than a **slow** film.

Splice: the **cut** or edit where two pieces of film are physically joined together.

Splicer: device used to cut and tape film.

Sprocket: a gear inside a film camera or projector that engages **sprocket holes** on the film to move it through the camera or projector.

Sprocket holes: a uniform row of holes along one or both edges of the film, engaged by the **sprocket wheel** and the **pull-down claw** in order to advance the film through the camera or projector.

Sprocket wheel: the toothed wheel that drives the film through the camera or projector by engaging the film's **perforations**.

Standard-definition: (**SD**) video formats with fewer than 720 horizontal lines of resolution. Standard-definition video is being replaced by **high-definition** video.

Static shot: a shot in which the camera does not move.

Stop: 1) each of the **f-stop** numbers. 2) the difference between one f-stop and the next.

Stop down: to close the lens iris.

Storyboard: a drawn version of a **script** or **treatment** resembling a comic strip; used to pre-visualize a **scene** or a film.

Super-8: a film **format** in which the strip of film is eight millimeters wide but with a larger frame area than regular **8mm** film.

Super-16: **16mm** film shot with a modified camera (using **single-perf film**) to create a frame area with a 1.66:1 **aspect ratio**.

Supercardioid microphone: same as **hypercardioid microphone**.

S-video: a video connection that carries **luminance** and **chrominance** information separately, sometimes referred to as a **Y-C** connection.

Sync head: a special head in an analog tape recorder that records a **sync pulse** on the tape.

Synchronization rights: for a musical composition, the right to use the actual recording of the music.

Sync pulse: a reference signal recorded onto the magnetic tape and used for synchronization in analog double-system film shooting.

Sync sound: audio that is matched exactly to picture during both shooting and editing.

Tail: the end of a reel of film. Film that has not been rewound is "tails out."

Take: same as **camera take**.

Take-up reel: the reel on which the film is stored after running through the camera or projector.

Tape recorder: a device that records an audio signal onto magnetic tape so that it can be played back later.

Telecine: a device used to electronically transfer film to **videotape**.

Telephoto lens: a lens with a long **focal length** which will capture only a narrow angle of the view in front of it; the more telephoto a lens is, the greater its magnifying power.

Temporal compression: a type of video **compression** that discards some of the video frames and creates "predicted frames" to replace them upon **decompression**.

Theatrical exhibition: the release of a film in movie theaters.

Three-CCD camera: same as **three-chip camera**.

Three-chip camera: a video camera that uses a prism to break the incoming light into separate red, green and blue portions, each of which is recorded by a separate chip.

Tilt: a camera move in which the camera pivots up or down along a vertical axis.

Time lapse: a type of cinematography in which single frames are taken at regular timed intervals, resulting in extremely **fast motion**.

Timing: adjustments made to the color and exposure of individual shots when a film is printed.

Track: in a **non-linear editing system** timeline a track is a visual representation of an audio or video **clip**, indicating the clip's duration and position within the edited sequence.

Tracking shot: a **dolly** shot in which the camera moves with a moving subject, keeping it in frame.

Trailers: commercials for films usually created using footage taken from the film.

Treatment: a written description of a film's concept and structure; in a **narrative** film the treatment would be a scene-by-scene description of the plot.

Treble: high-frequency sound.

Trims: film frames cut off of the **head** and **tail** of shots during editing.

Tripod: a three-legged support on which the camera rests.

Tungsten-balanced: 1) in the case of a light source, one which emits light of the tungsten **color temperature** (3200 K). 2) in the case of a color film stock, one which is manufactured to reproduce color correctly when exposed under illumination of the tungsten color temperature.

Undercranking: shooting at a **frame rate** slower than that at which the film or video is later shown, resulting in **fast motion** on the screen.

Underexpose: to allow too little light to hit the film or the video chip.

Unmotivated light: light which does not have a logical source shown or suggested in a scene.

Video art: experimental video work that exploits the unique characteristics of the video format.

Video dailies: a low-quality film-to-video transfer containing special information used for computerized editing of a film.

Video deck: a **VTR** that is a separate piece of machinery from the video camera.

Video installation: a type of video presentation that typically involves multiple screens or an assemblage of various media.

Video noise: random, usually unwanted areas of brightness and color in a video image.

Video switcher: a device that can select signals from multiple **source decks** to create effects and transitions.

Videotape: a flexible material, coated on one side with a magnetically-sensitive **oxide**, used in a **videotape recorder**.

Videotape recorder: (**VTR**) a machine that records the video signal onto videotape so that it can be played at a later date.

Viewer: a film editing device consisting of a screen, gate, feed reel and take-up reel that allows the filmmaker to look at film footage and select and edit shots.

Voice-over: speech that is heard on a **soundtrack** while the speaker or narrator is not seen.

VTR: see **videotape recorder**.

Wavelength: the distance one cycle of a sine wave covers, from crest to crest or from trough to trough.

White balance: adjusting the sensitivity of the red, green and blue color components in a video camera to change the overall color of the image.

Wide-angle lens: a lens of short **focal length** that will capture a wide angle of the view in front of it.

Wipe: a transition in which one shot replaces another shot by progressively replacing an area of the image until the outgoing shot has been completely replaced by the incoming shot.

Workprint: a frame-for-frame copy of a camera original film used for editing.

Y-C: same as **S-video**.

Zebra stripes: a pattern of diagonal stripes that appear on areas of a video viewfinder image that exceed a certain brightness level.

Zoom lens: a lens with a continuously variable range of **focal lengths**, usually ranging from a **wide-angle** position to a **telephoto** position; a lens that is capable of a "zoom" effect.

Index

About The Authors

The authors of *Shot by Shot: A Practical Guide to Filmmaking*, John Cantine, Susan Howard and Brady Lewis, are all active independent filmmakers with many years of combined experience teaching film and video production at every level. They are all members of the faculty of Pittsburgh Filmmakers' School of Film, Photography and Digital Media. **John Cantine** received his M.F.A. in Film Production from Ohio University. He is an independent video artist, freelance editor and script consultant. **Susan Howard**'s B.A. is in Film Production from Penn State University, and she has worked on film and television projects as diverse as the low-budget splatter feature *Street Trash* and *Mr. Rogers' Neighborhood*. She is the Director of the youth media program at Pittsburgh Filmmakers/Pittsburgh Center for the Arts. **Brady Lewis**, Pittsburgh Filmmakers' Director of Education, has a B.F.A. from New York University. His experimental work has been recognized by many regional and national film production grants, screenings and festival awards. He also completed a feature-length film, *Daddy Cool*, in 2003.

About Pittsburgh Filmmakers

Pittsburgh Filmmakers, one of the oldest and largest media centers in the United States, has provided support and equipment access to artists working in film, video, photography and digital media since 1971. Serving as the most prominent exhibitor of American independent films and foreign films in western Pennsylvania, Filmmakers operates three theaters and annually hosts the two-week Three Rivers Film Festival. Pittsburgh Filmmakers' School of Film, Photography and Digital Media is an accredited institutional member of the National Association of Schools of Art and Design (NASAD), offering a comprehensive curriculum encompassing film production, digital video production, photography, digital media and film history and theory. Pittsburgh Filmmakers merged with Pittsburgh Center for the Arts in 2006.

For more information on Pittsburgh Filmmakers and its programs or on *Shot by Shot: A Practical Guide to Filmmaking*, visit us on the web at ***www.pghfilmmakers.org***.